The Sauna

The Sauna

by ROB ROY

Chelsea Green Publishing Company / White River Junction, Vermont

Illustration by Sally Onopa on page 65 first appeared in Rodales's *New Shelter* (February 1982). Used by permission of the artist.

Book design by Christopher Kuntze

Printed in the United States of America
99   98   2   3   4   5

The information contained in this book is true and complete to the best of our knowledge. Due to the variability of local conditions, materials, skills, sites, and other factors, Chelsea Green Publishing Company and the author disclaim all liability for personal injury, property damage, or loss from actions inspired by the information in this book.

Library of Congress Cataloging-in-Publication Data
   Roy, Rob, 1947–
   The sauna / Rob Roy.
      p.   cm.
   Includes bibliographical references and index.
   ISBN 0–930031–87–3
      I. Sauna—Design and construction.   I. Title.
   TH4761.R69   1996
   690'.89—dc 20   96–27610

For

DARIN SCOT ROY

a great little sauna-mate

ACKNOWLEDGMENTS

This book was fun to research and to write, but it wouldn't be as thorough if it were not for the help of some fine people. Sincere thanks to Charlie Nurnberg of Sterling Publishing Company for permission to use photos and drawings that originally appeared in my earlier book, *Complete Book of Cordwood Masonry Housebuilding*. Brotherly thanks to George Roy for preparing a list of sauna suppliers. Thanks and hugs for friends Cliff and Jackie Shockey and Stephen, Robin, and Merlin Larsen for photos of their own saunas. Loving thanks to Jaki for clerical help, great meals, and doing more than her share of dishwashing during the last few weeks of writing. Saunaly thanks to all my steammates who helped me test new innovations at our Earthwood sauna. Neighborly thanks to Jeremiah Lee for his drawing of the yet-to-be oval sauna. Löyly thanks to Erkki Lindstrom, Vince Paladino, Ron Chartier, Frank DeFazio, John Gunderson, John Lysaker, Catherine Hanson, Ted Heikkinen, Mattie Kaups, V. S. Choslowsky, and all the other sauna suppliers and enthusiasts across North America who helped me with my researches. Thanks to Rachael Cohen and Ben Watson for their helpful early reading of the manuscript, editor David Dobbs for improving my written thoughts, and to the Chelsea Green production staff, who transformed piles of files of assorted artwork, photographs, slides, and text into a beautiful book. And, finally, special thanks to Jim Schley and Stephen Morris, without whom the idea for this book would never have germinated.

Contents

Introduction

THIS BOOK is about sauna. Most people know that sauna is a type
of sweat bath, even if they're a little shaky on the pronunciation,
which is *sow-nuh*, not *sawn-ah*. But the book also has a lot to do with
cordwood masonry, a building style that sounds like a contradiction in
terms, something that would make a stone or brick mason shudder.
Wood and masonry? "Can't do it," says the old-timer. "Like oil and
water. They don't mix." He's wrong, of course. And if he was a really
old old-timer, particularly from Wisconsin or Canada's Ottawa Valley,
he'd say, "Cordwood masonry? Sure, lots of that around here. Houses
and barns were built that way 'round the turn of the century. Many are
still standin'. Only we call 'em stovewood walls."

Or *firewood* walls, or *stackwall,* or *log-end* walls. Whatever, this old-
timer is referring to an ancient technique — as old as saunas themselves (which are at least 1,000 years old) — by which walls are built of
short logs laid widthwise in the wall, much as a rank of firewood (or
cordwood) is stacked. The wall gets its structural integrity and unique
thermal characteristics from a special insulated mortar matrix woven
throughout the wall. To complete the lexicography, the individual
masonry units, the pieces of wood, have been variously called *log-ends*,
log butts, even *blocks.*

Sauna requires much less elucidation, but it is important to note
that it is a Finnish word referring to a building in which a particular
kind of bathing takes place. The Finns might add that, besides bathing,
the sauna experience has a whole range of additional values, as noted
in Chapter One. The Finns also have a verb, *saunoa,* which doesn't
translate directly into English. We must speak of "taking a sauna." In
general, the kind of bathing that takes place in a sauna is a heavy per-
spiring in hot, dry air, interspersed with invigorating charges of steam,
and culminating in a cooling shower or dip in a pond, lake, or pool.

There is more to it than that, as we will see, but this will suit our purpose for the moment.

The sauna must be capable of holding a tremendous heat in the fabric of the building and in the stove and rocks immediately surrounding the stove. In Finland, much care is taken to "season" or "ripen" the sauna prior to use. This means firing the stove several hours before it is to be used, in order to charge the fabric with heat. The result of ripening the sauna is to produce a "soft" heat, as opposed to a harsh radiant heat. A properly seasoned sauna can last several hours at the desired heat without constant firing of the stove. This is very important to the total sauna experience, the comfort and the relaxation, as described in chapter seven.

And here is where the cordwood masonry and sauna make their marvelous intersection in time and space. Cordwood walls combine exactly the characteristics required of a sauna: They have a high insulation value. They have tremendous thermal mass for the storage of heat. And, they are porous, so they absorb steam quickly, a characteristic highly valued by the Finns. That they are also fun, easy, and inexpensive to construct transforms the building experience into almost the same spiritual plane as the actual sauna experience. But, to me, leaving all considerations of function, practicality, and economy aside, a small cordwood building just *looks* like a sauna. It is made from the same materials used to fire it. (Leftover or reject log-ends can provide the first ceremonial firing.) It harmonizes with the surrounding landform, because it is made from indigenous materials. It even accents the texture and appearance of the woodpile nearby.

At its highest level, sauna is, indeed, a spiritual experience. And the building in which this experience occurs should be no less blessed. In my view, the creativity of design possible with cordwood masonry contributes mightily to this sacred atmosphere. Such special features as meditation points, shelves, and patterns of bottle-ends can be included easily and naturally. Even in its simplest and purest form, cordwood masonry's textural joy, warm colors, and pleasing relief contribute to the right effect, whether the builder is creative or not.

But if the builder has shown the imagination necessary to tackle a cordwood sauna, chances are the creativity is there, too. Go and have a ball. Send me a picture of the finished job, and I'll send you a Master Mortar Stuffer's Certificate (see p. 186 for address). That's a promise.

And most important of all: Enjoy your sauna!

The Sauna

The Log End Sauna.

The Earthwood Sauna.

· 1 ·

About Saunas

SINCE THE SAUNA first invaded American shores as a status symbol in the early 1960s, there has been no shortage of books, articles, and technical papers published about saunas, and I've read a substantial chunk of them to prepare for this book. Some of this literature is illuminating, some humorous, some just plain claptrap. Many of these writings, however, are personal to those who wrote them, and this is as it must be, because the sauna experience is highly personal, much as our experiences in, say, literature, politics, or beer. I will follow this same approach, and leave it to others to decide if my commentary is illuminating, humorous, or just plain claptrap. Fact and myth are hard to differentiate when the subject is sauna, particularly its history, legend, health benefits (or risks), and the highly opinionated area of The Right Way to Take a Sauna.

Either you're a sauna person or you're not. If you're reading this book, you probably are one. This book will show you how to build a low-cost, high-quality sauna that you'll feel very good about using. If you aren't sure whether you're a sauna person (saunas, like Steppenwolf's Magic Theatre, are "Not For Everyone") then put this book back on the shelf right now and go take a sauna somewhere: a health club, good hotel, neighbor. Don't know the neighbor? People with saunas are friendly. Knock on the door. Far-fetched? Listen. I'll tell you how I became a sauna person, over thirty years ago.

THE AUTHOR AND THE SAUNA:
A PERSONAL ODYSSEY

When I was still in high school, I started my first business, a water-skiing school in Webster, Massachusetts, on the shores of beautiful Lake *Chargoggagoggmanchaugagoggchaubunagungamaugg*. (There will be a quiz.) I plied my trade at a motel called Treasure Island, which had a sauna and a pool. After a hard day of teaching skiing or hanging around the beach waiting for customers, I would unwind my stressed out sixteen-year-old body in the sauna, at about 180 degrees Fahrenheit. Sometimes one of my friends, students, or co-instructors would join me. It was a typical American redwood sauna of the day, electrically heated, very dry. I didn't know anything about saunas, but I knew what I liked.

At nineteen, I left home to see the world. I just kept heading east until I got back to the point of beginning. En route, I stopped for a couple of days in Iceland and stayed at the Loftleider Hotel in Reykjavik. The hotel's sauna was maintained at a balmy 220 degrees F., being 8 degrees above boiling temperature. The routine was a few minutes in the sauna, and then a plunge (a climb down a ladder, actually, but "plunge" sounds more dramatic) into a cubicle of cold water about the size and shape of a telephone kiosk set into the floor. Repeat two or three times. Compared to the Treasure Island sauna, this was much closer to the true Finnish experience. (Finland, of course, is the sauna's homeland, and you'll be learning a few important Finnish words in this chapter. They are important not only because they have no direct English translations, but because they are really good words to know if you ever get to Finland, where the sauna is the social meeting place.)

At twenty-one, I bought two attached and nearly dilapidated cottages in the Northwest Highlands of Scotland, sitting on a quarter-acre of land overlooking the Cromarty Firth. The twenty-four hundred dollars for this property, and half of the seven thousand dollars renovation expense, was money that was supposed to send me to college. Harold Wilson's socialist government was kind enough to fork up the other half by way of a housing grant.

"Ye might as well hang for a sheep as a lamb," goes the Highland saying, so I decided to incorporate a small sauna into the bathroom, right next to a shower cubicle. As even showers were a rarity in Scotland at that time, it was no surprise that information was lacking locally about building a sauna. However, the electrical contractor knew of an American (the place was fairly crawlin' with the beasts) who had bought and renovated a castle on the Black Isle just a few miles away. I boldly made my way up to the imposing entrance and knocked on the oak door. Mr. Robinson, the new laird of this ancient manor, was kind enough to show me around the castle and particularly the sauna. He told me what kind of wood he had used for the sauna cabinet (Czechoslovakian red pine) and many other helpful details. So, you shouldn't be afraid to beg a bath from those rich neighbors with the sauna by their pool. They'll probably join you.

By the way, I never went to college. Instead, Mountrich Cottage turned out to be the grubstake for the homestead and (eventually) building school that my wife Jaki and I have been caught up with for the past 24 years. But that's another book.

The Sauna in the Highlands

My government grant agreement required that I get bids from at least two masons, joiners, plumbers, and electricians. My contributions to the project were in the fields of design and destruction. I drew the original renovation plans (refined by a local architect) and helped the joiner (carpenter) and mason (still a good friend 25 years later) with the tear-out. The place needed almost total gutting. Deteriorated lath and plaster abounded like you wouldn't believe. Other tear-out was necessary to widen windows, a code requirement. The home had no insulation, a common situation in Scotland at that time.

The joiner built the sauna to my design, about 4 feet wide, 6 feet long, and 7 feet high. Rather than spend big pounds for a special sauna heater from Finland, I bought an inexpensive 3-kilowatt electric space heater, which my electrician friend adapted for my purpose by defeating the built-in thermostat with a new bypass switch. Without this modification, the sauna would never get warmer than about 80 degrees F.

The sauna was great. I introduced a lot of people to the joys of saunas in the five years I owned Mountrich Cottage. We would use it after work, after evenings at the squash club, even after the pub closed at ten o'clock. (This latter circumstance, mixing alcohol and the sauna, is not advised, as we will see. Do as I say, not as I did in my young and foolish days.)

One famous night—the evening of the longest day, when it never gets totally dark in the North of Scotland—a few of the lads and I decided to climb Ben Wyvis, which at 3400 feet is the area's most commanding mountain. We arrived at the top in a blizzard, with sleet hitting the backs of our pants legs horizontally. We had planned to pitch a tent and observe the sunrise about 2:30 a.m. Well, not only was there going to be no sunrise, but the keeper of the tent had forgotten to pack tent pegs. I was as cold and wet and miserable as I've ever been, before or since. Back we trudged, for a couple of sodden hours, to the Garve Hotel, where this silly expedition had started. A half hour later, at Mountrich, we fired up the sauna (actually, I flipped the electric switch) and we cooked up some bacon and eggs while the room heated up to 160 degrees. We actually ate our breakfast in the sauna (another no-no) and I have to say that this was probably the most appreciated sauna and breakfast that I have ever experienced. Quite a night. I can't imagine how we would have dried out and brought our body temperatures up without that sauna.

On a different night, maybe one of those after the pub, I enjoyed a leisurely sauna and went to bed relaxed. When I woke the next morning, I instantly realized that I had forgotten to turn off the sauna heater. The thermostat had been bypassed, you'll recall. I got to the sauna so fast that I'm surprised I didn't leave my silhouette in the bedroom panel door on the way through, like Donald Duck in a cartoon. I opened the sauna door to find the thermometer pegged at 310 degrees Fahrenheit! The Czechoslovakian red pine was oozing sticky pitch from the walls and ceiling. This was an oven, no longer a sauna!

Days later, when the room had cooled, I scraped the hardened pitch away and sanded the woodwork as good as new. The net effect was a great improvement to my sauna. Prior to this inadvertent "seasoning," the walls would occasionally get sticky with pitch. No more. Every last drop of pitch was forever bled away that night. I was lucky. I cannot, in conscience, advise you to defeat the thermostat in a sauna heater. Don't repeat my mistakes. Go and find your own.

(Postscript: Back in 1969, when I moved in to Mountrich, I put three cool and colorful Swiss mountain scenes on the walls of the sauna. I had saved them from an expired calendar. In October of 1996, Jaki and I went back to Scotland and stayed at the cottage next door to the one I had renovated. We got to know the new owners of Mountrich Cottage, Angus and Lorraine McLeod, during our week's stay, and, one day, Angus gave us a tour of our old place. Not a word of a lie: but the three calendar pictures of Swiss mountains had not moved from their original places on the wall, despite the McLeods being the third owners of the cottage after us! I felt pretty good about that. And I know that next time we go back to visit, I'll have a sauna again in Old Number One, for Auld Lang Syne.)

The Saunas at Log End

Jaki and I moved to West Chazy, New York, in 1975, and built Log End Cottage, the first house we had actually built ourselves from scratch. We combined elements of the old English black and white timber-framed houses, a certain Scandinavian chalet exterior appearance, and that (almost) uniquely North American building technique, cordwood masonry. There was no way we were going to live without our sauna, which had become a regular part of our lives. We incorporated an indoor sauna into a corner of Log End Cottage, right off the bathroom, heated with a woodstove welded of ¼-inch plate steel. The two exterior walls were cordwood masonry, and the two interior walls were framed with 2 × 4s, insulated with fiberglass, and covered with rough boards and log slabs from a sawmill.

The Log End Cottage sauna had redwood 2 × 6 planks for benches, a choice I would not make again, for ecological reasons, as well as for practicality and economy, as will be discussed in the construction chapters. The sauna was about 5 by 8 feet, with a 7-foot ceiling. The stove was in a corner and the adjacent walls were protected by asbestos board. The sauna worked very well; 180-degree temperatures were no problem to maintain. The only drawback was that the sauna tended to heat up the house quite a bit, which wasn't so bad in the winter, but made summer baths out of the question. Part of the reason for this heat build-up was that the sauna stove's stovepipe vented through a brick opening in the wall and into the main kitchen area before exiting the home through the cathedral ceiling. Stovepipes give off a lot of heat. Still, we used the sauna frequently, except in July and August, and it was every bit as good as the one at Mountrich. In fact, with the wood heat and rustic walls, it had decidedly more "atmosphere."

Next we built Log End Cave, an underground home with cordwood masonry for all the above-grade walls (which, with the large south-facing windows, wasn't a whole lot of cordwood masonry). This home too had a sauna, but it was never completed with proper benches. We took exactly one sauna in it, to test it, and then the room became used for storage, which was sorely needed. It was only fair as a sauna. As at Log End Cottage, the bath was in a corner, but the two

1-1. Log End Sauna.

"exterior" walls were 12-inch concrete block, not cordwood, and they tended to absorb the heat from the stove. It took a long time to "season" the sauna, and it lacked ambience. Concrete block walls, even made smooth with surface-bonding cement, just don't have the character, relief, and visual warmth of cordwood masonry. Like Howard Hughes' Spruce Goose, the Cave Sauna flew just once. By this time we had decided to build an outdoor sauna between the Cottage and the Cave, a place where occupants of either house could go to get away from the telephone, and mundane household chores, and without overheating the home at the same time. Thus was born Log End Sauna, described in detail in chapter three. This was definitely our most successful sauna yet. It offered the added attraction of getting away to someplace special, a feature not present in any of our previous saunas, and the atmosphere was close to magical. The heavy post-and-beam frame, the split cedar fencerail log-ends, and the earth roof all contributed to a charming appearance from without. There was no electricity, so evening saunas were always conducted with subdued light, usually candles. And we had two large thermalpane windows facing south for a good view into the woods. We incorporated an antechamber for dressing as well as a place for washing down under a solar shower. Although we sold Log End several years ago, the building has been in continuous use as a sauna since 1979.

The Earthwood Sauna

We built the round Earthwood sauna in 1980, and still use it regularly. The cylindrical shape allows the building to be easily heated, and imparts a sense of womblike comfort. It is my favorite sauna, of all I have experienced throughout the world. (I admit to bias. The sauna that you build will suit you better than mine ever could. This is as it should be.) Although the Earthwood sauna does not have its own attached dressing room, it is only ten feet from the house. We can use the solar room or the adjacent downstairs den as a changing room and relaxation area.

I'm not trying to impress you with the number of saunas I've built. The point is that every one of these saunas has been different and has contributed in some way to my perception of what a sauna is and should be. Almost everyone who builds a sauna is pleased with the result (in fact, I can't think of the exception), be it made from an old wooden silo, recycled boards, cordwood, whatever. Build it stout, insulate it well, make it safe, and you won't go wrong.

A LITTLE HISTORY

The sauna in its classic form has a long association with the Finnish people. How long? A thousand years without question, for there are written accounts that old which describe a sauna not unlike the modern Finnish sauna. But many Finns claim a two thousand-year association, and I certainly have little reason or inclination to doubt them. When something has maintained as esteemed a position in society as the sauna has in Finland for at least a millenium, what's the point of quibbling about the odd century or two?

To be sure, other societies have had similar customs. Dry heat as well as steam baths both had their advocates in ancient Rome, and many public baths, such as some I have visited along Hadrian's wall in northern England, incorporated both dry and wet rooms in the same establishment. The Greeks, the Turks, the Russians, the Japanese, the Native Americans, and others have all adhered to their own twist on the ancient bathing ritual. A long personal interest in Europe's neolithic period (our sauna overlooks a megalithic stone circle) leads me to the conclusion that the ritual of ceremonial bathing dates back thousands of years. The sweat lodges of pre-Columbian America may be equally as old.

(For those interested in the history and folklore of sauna in Finland, I recommend *Sauna: The Finnish Bath* by H. J. Viherjuuri. For a look at ancient Native American sweat lodge customs, and the close parallels between the sweat lodge and the sauna, see *The Sauna Book* [1977]. These books and other materials about sauna are included in the Annotated Bibliography.)

The Smoke Sauna

Did the ancients really have this deep concern about health and cleanliness? It's doubtful. Many of the rituals involved smoke in the Native American sweat lodges or even the early Finnish "smoke saunas," hardly a healthy atmosphere. Assisted by pipes, others mainlined other kinds of smoke during the experience, more as an aid to spiritual perception than for physical well-being. (No, I don't advise this either, but stay with me. I'm not a total fuddy duddy.)

The smoke sauna warrants a close look, because it is a direct ancestor of the modern Finnish sauna experience. The earliest saunas may have been underground, an extension, perhaps, of cave life. In any case, underground or above grade (the surface saunas were generally constructed of horizontal logs), the science of chimneys was little known in ancient times. The "firebox," or, perhaps more accurately, "firepit," was typically constructed with walls of stone arched carefully over the top of the place where the fire was set. The fire was lit and fed by the fire keeper, who would crawl in once in a while to stoke the flames. The living fire directly heated the rocks to high temperature, almost glowing red. The by-product, of course, was smoke, which filled the room, coating walls, ceiling, and any benches or platforms (and probably the fire keeper himself) with black soot. Ancient reports are sketchy, but it seems that the smoke was then let out of the room, leaving the very hot rocks to continue heating the sauna for hours afterward. Some authorities have the keeper washing the benches with water prior to the bathers taking their places, though other sources omit reference to this nicety.

No less an authority than H. J. Viherjuuri, author of *Sauna: The Finnish Bath* and considered to be "the father of modern sauna," says, "The old smoke sauna was the most common type in rural Finland until the end of the nineteenth century." During the twentieth century, thanks largely to the demands of fire insurance companies, a firebox enclosed with sheet metal and having a chimney became the norm, although Viherjuuri reckons that any authentic sauna should have at least a background fragrance of smoke.

Very few advocates of the original smoke sauna (or "savusauna") can still be found, although I had a long conversation with one strong advocate recently. Vince Paladino of Riverhead, New York, believes that the savusauna is the best and the only truly authentic sauna. Vince even offered to come up to West Chazy and baptize the Earthwood sauna with smoke, but I declined the invitation. I asked Vince how such a chimneyless fire was stoked, and his response was that you opened the door quickly, crawled in, threw your charge of hardwood logs into the stone-lined firepit, and retreated. All in one breath, I presume.

The "black houses" on the Western Isles of Scotland were stone cottages with walls four or five feet thick. The roofs were very thick, of a kind of straw thatch over rafters. Fires of peat burned in the hearth, often just a shallow pit in the middle of the floor. There were no chimneys. The peat smoke had to find a way out through the straw. It's no mystery why they were called "black houses." While those on display to tourists in Skye and Lewis have a certain charm, the reality is that life expectancy for the inhabitants was less than 40 years. No thank you; I have become a great fan of the chimney (call me a "chimney fan" if you must) and even admit partiality to those with a good draft.

In defense of the ancients, remember that it is only in the last half of the 20th century that the health detriments of smoke have been generally accepted. Some tobacco executives still insist that smoking is not harmful to health, and millions of people seem to believe it.

Löyly: The Sacred Steam

Yet we must not dismiss old customs out of hand, or we will lose contact with much of the spiritual, mystical, and ritualistic side of the sauna, which makes it so much more than a bath. H. J. Viherjuuri:

> Many strange beliefs and superstitions are connected with the sauna and with bathing customs. The ancient Finns believed, like many other primitive peoples, that fire came from heaven and that therefore it was sacred. The fireplace and the pile of stones were altars. The sauna was a place for the worship of the dead, who were supposed to return gladly, even after death, to so pleasant a place.

Now, you need to know another very important Finnish word,

löyly, pronounced "low-lu." Today, löyly is what Finns call the steam that rises from the stones, but its original connotation signified "spirit," even "life." Many consider löyly to be the soul of the sauna, and it has a connection with the sacred that goes back too far to date. It was thought that the löyly could drive diseases and evil humors out of the body. "Even unhappy love affairs could be settled by the sauna," reports Viherjuuri.

There's definitely something to it. I don't know if its the löyly, but something about a sauna soothes the troubled mind and promotes good fellowship. A past president of Finland, Urho Kekkonen, once said, "There are no ministers, VIPs, laborers, or lumberjacks on the sauna platform, only sauna mates" (as quoted by Jon R. Luoma in *Audubon*). Former Secretary of State James Baker once took off his clothes and joined the equally naked president of Kazakhstan in a sauna to talk about the fate of the former Soviet Union. This went on until 3 A.M. My theory on this ability of the sauna to promote honest conversation is that it's pretty hard to be dishonest when you are totally naked. There's nothing to hide. Urho Kekkonen was right when he called the sauna "a great leveler."

Like so many Finnish citizens born in the sauna over the centuries, the idea for this book was given birth there. Chelsea Green publisher Stephen Morris and editor-in-chief Jim Schley came over to Earthwood in December of 1995 to finalize arrangements on another book we had been discussing for some time. Our discussions took place partially in the sauna, where Jim suggested a book on building a sauna. It is clear to me that had we not taken a sauna that day, this book would not exist. Then the reader would probably not build his or her cordwood sauna and who knows how that would change your life, that of others, maybe the whole history of the planet. That löyly can be potent stuff!

Smoke House, Drying Room, Birthing Chamber, Mortuary, Temporary Shelter . . .

Historically, the sauna was multifunctional. Besides the weekly (usually Saturday) family bath, the building served many other purposes: smoking and curing meat, doing laundry, drying thatch, malting barley, breaking flax, and drying fish nets, just to name a few. Massage and blood-letting took place there. In olden times, a bride and bridegroom took a sauna together before going to the altar. (One wonders if many minds were changed by this custom.) The sick were sometimes nursed to health in the sauna, and the dead washed and made ready for burial. Besides many births taking place in the sauna, Viherjuuri tells us that "many an old man and women (were) carried there to die." No wonder the sauna plays such an important part in Finnish life. No wonder we read time and again that there are two religions in Finland: the Church and the Sauna.

When Finns settled in the United States, especially in Minnesota and Wisconsin in the 19th century, they brought an Old Country strategy with them: They would build the sauna before the house. The sauna served as a temporary shelter to live in while they built their house, and could serve several of the other functions useful to farmsteading. One wonders if they would clear all their personal belongings out of the sauna once in a while, in order to use it for its primary purpose, or if they waited until the house was completed before firing it up for the first time. Certainly, a bath would be more than welcome by that time. Writer Jon R. Luoma tells us that another custom was carried to America:

> Well into this century, many used the family sauna as a delivery room, as had their forebears in the old country. It was clean, it afforded privacy and its warmth (not stoked to full blast) was believed to help relax a mother in labor. There probably were other reasons, too, reasons reaching back into something like tribal memory, reasons that had to do with sacrament and spirit.

If the sauna is just a bath, then Buckingham Palace is just a house.

THE SAUNA AND YOUR HEALTH

If you think the sauna history recounted above is fuzzy, be prepared for all the conflicting reports that you are bound to hear about the health benefits—and risks—of the sauna. I will try to help you through it, but ultimately I can only report what I have read, giving greater weight to statements reported again and again from a variety of respectable sources and lesser weight to what seem to be unsubstantiated claims. And I will share some of my own personal experiences and let you file them under illumination, humor, or claptrap.

Fact or Fiction?

You may have heard: Saunas are a great way to lose weight. Reality check: You'll lose one to three pounds in a typical sauna, but you'll gain it back as soon as you drink one to three pounds of water, juice, pop, or beer. Basically, we're all bags of water (90 percent of our body weight), and the bags are made of our largest organ, the epidermis (skin to the layman). When we sweat, this bag springs thousands of leaks and a few pints of water drip out. So, while some wrestlers have been known to spend an hour in a sauna to "make weight" (with what other negative effects on their bodies we can't fully imagine), experts agree that if you want to lose weight, eat less (particularly less fat) and exercise more. The sauna won't help.

You may have heard: Sauna is good for your skin. Reality: consensus says it probably is. A good flow of perspiration can carry out dirt, stale body oil, dead skin, sebum, and certain blood chemicals such as sodium and electrolytes, so some internal cleansing might be considered to be taking place. Viherjuuri says (and I tend to agree): "Induced perspiration is the best known means of cleansing the skin." From experience, I find that a good sweat in a sauna works particularly well in loosening hard-to-displace grime, oils, pitches, and the like that come from hard or dirty work. It seems to drive the dirt out of one's skin from the inside. As an adolescent, I was bothered by acne attacks. Saunas definitely improved my condition, but certainly didn't cure it.

You may have heard: Saunas increase (or decrease) blood pressure and the risk of heart attack. Reality check: mixed. A standard warning by manufacturers of sauna and hot tub equipment advises those with respiratory and heart diseases and those troubled by blood pressure abnormalities to check with a doctor before using said equipment. Problem is that doctors won't all agree with each other on this issue. Most today will probably take the safe route: "Don't use the sauna." Cynically, we might say that the manufacturers (and the doctors) are just trying to protect themselves from lawsuits. But there is more to it than that.

Your heart works harder in a sauna. No question about it. Heart rate can increase from around 72 beats per minute to anywhere from 100 to 160 beats. The load of the heart in the sauna corresponds to light physical work or to fever in moderate degree. Blood circulation also increases, but not necessarily blood pressure, because the heat simultaneously dilates the blood vessel walls, which accommodates the increased blood flow. Circulation could double, from around 5 to 7 quarts per minute all the way up to 11 to 13 quarts. This is your body's reaction to the great heat. The heart pumps more blood to the surface of the skin, trying to bring down the temperature. A healthy or normal heart can handle these stresses, and might even benefit from the cardiovascular workout. What about an unhealthy heart? A doctor's consultation is the safest course, but be prepared for an answer you might not want to hear.

Dr. Ilkka Vuori, in *Annals of Clinical Research* (Special Issue on Sauna, 1988), concludes his well-researched and documented paper entitled "Sauna Bather's Circulation" with:

> Moderate sauna bathing causes a significant but usually well-tolerated hyperkinaemia and thus increased volume load but not pressure load to the heart. However, in unaccustomed subjects and in those with high sympathetic reactivity like very untrained persons and convalescent patients heart rate may increase and blood pressure decrease excessively causing symptoms even in ordinary bathing. . . . Additional stress like heavy meals and especially any great amount of alcohol has to be avoided. When the bather follows the simple guidelines, developed during centuries of tradition, and his own feelings, even an inexperienced bather can confidently enjoy a risk-free pleasurable experience.

In chapter seven I will return to these simple guidelines of which Dr. Vuori speaks.

A Couple of Cautions

Dr. Vuori's admonition introduces two important no-no's in the sauna: heavy eating and alcohol. Don't eat for an hour before going in the sauna (two hours in the case of a big meal). Why? Digestion requires a lot of blood. Getting hot in the sauna also creates a big demand in the epidermis for blood as a coolant. You might not have enough blood to do both jobs well, which subjects the heart to a lot of stress. I might add, though, from personal experience, that going into the sauna hungry isn't so great either. That empty feeling seems to be heightened and is rather uncomfortable. I enjoy saunas best about two or three hours after eating.

Okay, now for the second no-no, and it pains me to tell you, though I hope it doesn't pain you to hear it: No booze before or during the sauna! I can hear some of you saying, "So what?" or "Who cares?" Good for you. That's the right attitude. Others, like yours truly, my better half, and some of our friends, will be saying, "Bummer! There's nothing like a cold beer in the sauna." (Or hot tub.) Yeah, it tastes good. I know. Done it. But here's why it's a bad idea: Mixing alcohol with high temperatures can give you a false idea about just how hot you are, and, in the worst case, might put you to sleep. Also, the impact of a unit of alcohol can be up to four times as powerful in the sauna environment. Carlton Hollander, in his book *How to Build a Sauna*, says, "Alcohol is definitely not recommended prior to a sauna, since it works as a depressant, with a quick flash of energy leading into a state where the blood is moving slowly and the nerve endings are literally shutting down. The alcohol tends to detract from the total benefit of the sauna experience." Finally, some yahoos can't seem to help overindulging in alcohol, with the result that the healthy sauna soon turns into a dangerous heat tolerance competition.

Now the good news. It's perfectly okay to drink water in the sauna to help replace the fluids you lose through perspiration. After a few minutes of rest in the relaxation room, it's okay to have a beer or two. My advice, though, is to drink a glass of water first, otherwise you'll think you've inhaled that first beer. And the really good news is that if you have a fondness for barley juice, as I do, you'll really appreciate it after a good session in the sauna.

The Sauna and Age

Children do fine in saunas, but their sweat glands are less developed than those of their parents, so they tend to prefer lower temperatures (the lower bench), or less time in the sauna. Son Darin, ten years old as I write, is just beginning to enjoy the sauna as a special family time. I think there is a bonding that takes place in the sauna that transcends age and sex. In Finland, of course, the sauna is an age-old family custom.

What about the sauna and the elderly? Well, in Finland, with a sauna for every five people, nearly 90 percent of people over eighty years of age are still taking sauna regularly. In fairness, though, we must remember that Finns have been accustomed to frequent saunas all their lives. For a person to start taking saunas at 65 or 70 could be a different matter. Again, the important consideration is the health of the individual, not the age. Dr. Jonathan L. Halperin, professor of internal medicine at Mount Sinai Medical Center in New York, is quoted as saying, "Moderate sauna use is safe for most older people, but diabetics and anyone being treated for heart or circulatory conditions should check with their doctor, particularly if they are taking medications" (quoted by Dorothy Berinstein in *Good Housekeeping*). And all people just starting out with the sauna, old or young, should go easy at first. Short sessions. Easy on the dips in ice water.

Ice and Snow Baths

What about those nuts we hear about who, during a sauna, jump into the lake through a hole in the ice, or roll around in the snow? Reports and advice vary widely. Viherjuuri enthuses:

> The feeling of well-being which follows the cold dip is undoubtedly one of the most delightful sensations which the human body can experience. For this reason, jumping in the lake can become almost a passion, and many sauna enthusiasts take as many as five dips into ice-cold water during one sauna visit. A jump into a hole in the ice after intense heat is not such terrifying sport as those who have never tried it allege.

Fair enough, but writer and sauna aficionado James McCommons has tried it, and disagrees: "Don't believe anyone who says it's healthy to cool down by rolling in the snow or jumping into a cold lake. I did it a few times for bragging rights, but the temperature extremes are a real shock to the system." Red Smith describes his experiences with saunas in Finland with his own inimitable wit: "The Gulf of Finland is colder than an Eskimo spinster. All feeling, however, had been left behind in the stewpot. The instant a guy hit the water, he turned numb; he suffered no more than a corpse."

Dr. Ilkka Vuori, in his paper entitled "Sauna Bather's Circulation," says, "If there is a risk of cardiovascular complications associated with sauna, it is greatest in sudden and intensive cooling following hot sauna. In particular, diving or immersion of the face in cold water should be avoided. In reality, severe untoward consequences are rare for at least two reasons: healthy subjects are not at risk and the individuals with manifest or latent cardiovascular diseases predisposed to the risk rarely expose themselves to severe conditions."

I would love to give you the last word based upon my lifetime of sauna experience, but, alas, I cannot. Yes, I have dipped in cold pools in Iceland, taken cold showers during saunas in Scotland, rolled in fluffy snowbanks in northern New York. It never comes easy. Sure it feels good, and puts a wide smile on your face. It also feels good to get back in the sauna. The best part about the cold plunge is that it cools your body and buys you more time in the "stewpot."

The Sauna and the Common Cold

Can the sauna cure (or cause) a cold? Mount Sinai's Dr. Halperin says that saunas may temporarily alleviate the symptoms of colds because the steam acts as a decongestant, but they won't shorten the duration (Berinstein, 1995). But regular use of the sauna might decrease the chance of getting colds in the first place. Veteran sauna bather and writer Leslie Li writes in *Health Magazine*:

> The results of a study conducted on schoolchildren in Germany, half of whom took saunas weekly, suggest that the heat increases resistance to viral infections, particularly the common cold.

In my younger days, I used to visit the sauna at the very first onset of a cold and I was (and remain) convinced that I was able to "sweat out" several colds in that way. I also remember trying the same thing a few years ago with no positive results. My theory, unproven, is that the success depends on the nature of the infection. And the hope of a "cure" is predicated upon the early application of the medicine, the sauna. Now, everybody is different, and I recognize that a positive attitude (faith?) may have as much to do with success as the sauna itself. Definitely don't take a sauna when your resistance or general health is at a low ebb. Will you catch a cold in the sauna? No, not unless an infected fellow bather sneezes all over you. One caution, though: Make sure you are fully dry and have stopped sweating before dressing and going out into the cold. The danger here is the possibility of chills from remaining in damp clothes.

The Sauna and Pregnancy

Should pregnant women use the sauna? Not according to Aubrey Milunsky, M.D., and Director of the Center for Human Genetics at Boston University Medical School. She cautions that exposure to intense heat during the first trimester increases the risk of birth defects such as spina bifida. Dr. Milunsky, quoted in *Good Housekeeping*, says, "Even though the additional risk is relatively small, the data should serve as a warning to pregnant women to avoid exposure to the high temperatures found in saunas, hot tubs, or steam rooms."

Dr. Milunsky's advice differs from the view from Finland. There, in a 1988 paper, Dr. K. Vaha-Eskeli and R. Erkkola of the Department of Obstetrics and Gynecology at the University of Turku report: "Up to 90 percent of pregnant women in Finland regularly visit the sauna until the expected time of delivery and Finnish women are confident that the sauna and pregnancy are compatible, a view that contrasts with many opinions abroad." In the same paper, incidentally, the authors report that sauna did not change the sperm count among male bathers.

It should be noted that Dr. Milunsky's commentary is more specific—and more recent—than that of the Finnish paper.

Will the sauna cause pregnancy? Not likely. At 180 degrees, sex will be about the furthest thing from your mind. But Carlton Hollander says:

> The sauna experience . . . will leave you feeling very much alive. Your senses will be sharpened, and your tactile sensitivity heightened. In the vernacular of today's world, you could define the state as being "turned on." But by then the sauna will be over and what you do is your own affair.

Other Health Claims

While wild health claims for the sauna are still unsubstantiated, there is agreement on a few benefits. Many doctors and patients report temporary relief from pain and inflammation connected with arthritis and rheumatism. Sports medicine experts use the sauna to relax sore muscles and treat minor aches after a strenuous workout. Asthma patients in Czechoslovakia take saunas to allow freer breathing, since the air sacs in the lungs dilate in the intense heat.

Finally, saunas are relaxing. They can help relax and loosen muscle tissue, decrease muscle tension, and increase flexibility by as much as 10 percent. Stress seems to evaporate in the sauna steam. While in the stove room, you are kind of forced to do nothing. Ideally, you should think nothing, too, and the stress-reducing benefits of meditation will begin to set in. Call it Sauna 202. Pseudo-psycho claptrap? Maybe. Psychology may have a lot to do with the feeling of well-being reported by sauna aficionados for hundreds of years on both sides of the Atlantic. After all, I have experienced similar benefits at a good English pub.

If it works, don't knock it.

· 2 ·

Cordwood Masonry

L IKE THE SAUNA, cordwood masonry has a long and colorful history, dating back at least 1000 years. The building technique may have Scandinavian roots. And, like the sauna, cordwood masonry was carried into the midwest in the mid-nineteenth century, particularly Wisconsin. I would like to report that saunas were built of cordwood masonry by Finns in the last century, but, as sensible a hypothesis as this may be, there is no field evidence to support it, nor even anecdotal accounts. Those interested in the history of cordwood masonry may wish to see my book *Complete Book of Cordwood Masonry Housebuilding: The Earthwood Method* and *Continental Cordwood Conference Collected Papers*, both listed in the bibliography.

WOOD ROT: THE MYTH

Much myth permeates the topic of cordwood masonry. The main myth is that cordwood masonry walls won't last. Relatives and uninitiated local builders may try to convince you that wood and mortar don't mix. "The wood will rot out!" "You can't do that!" "You're crazy!" They're myth-taken.

The distinguishing feature of cordwood masonry is that the log-ends are laid up transversely in the wall, much as a rank of firewood is stacked. Wood breathes wonderfully along end-grain, so moisture is never held for long by the wood fibers. The wall may get wet during a driving rainstorm, but within a few hours or days the wall will completely dry out.

Rot is caused not by water, nor even by wet wood, but by bacteria or fungi working on the wood in the presence of moisture. Constantly damp wood is what the little beasties like. If the wood goes wet and dry, wet and dry, the bacteria never get a foothold. Fenceposts rot at ground level, where soil stores moisture and provides the perfect climate for bacterial action. Split oak or cedar fence rails, exposed to the elements for decades—but off the ground—never seem to rot. A cordwood masonry wall breathes better than any other kind of wooden wall. Its short log-ends carry the moisture away along the longitudinal fibers of the wood. Built properly, a cordwood wall will last a century or longer, even in a sauna.

The four cardinal rules to ensure longevity are:

1. Put a good overhang on the building. I like 12 inches minimum, but 16 inches is not out of the question.

2. Keep the wood at least 6 inches off the ground, on a block, concrete, brick, or stone foundation.

3. Debark the wood so insects won't hang out beneath the bark.

4. Use good sound wood. Any log-ends that show the start of deterioration should be saved to help heat your sauna. Nothing is wasted with cordwood construction.

Weathering

The exterior surface of a cordwood masonry wall will weather. Most woods take on a silvery gray patina. Some, like white cedar, may be stained red by the sun, particularly on the south or west sides of the building. Others, like poplar, may turn quite black. Old poplar cordwood houses in Canada's prairie provinces are known as the Dalmation Houses because of the black spots the poplar log-ends make on the sun-bleached mortar background. Within the first year or two, this blackened appearance can be eliminated with either a 30 percent bleach solution applied with a brush, or, more tediously, with a 4,500 rpm disk sander. Use protective eyeglasses and a nose mask.

On the interior, cordwood walls will maintain their original appearance virtually forever. Our round house, called "Earthwood," looks the same on the inside as when the log-ends were mortared in 1980. The exterior has weathered somewhat, but there is no deterioration.

I advise people not to try to maintain the exterior of the cordwood wall to its original appearance. One of the great plusses to this building style is that it requires so little maintenance. Any kind of stain,

2-1. Log-ends can be brightened with a disk sander.

varnish, oil, or magic goop that you put on will require re-application a few years down the road. Sun and rain are powerful antagonists. You can't beat them, so it's better to just let the wall weather gracefully. It looks good. From a distance of 100 feet, people think it's a stone wall. Jaki and I hear strangers arguing about it at the head of the driveway.

ADVANTAGES OF A CORDWOOD SAUNA

You can build a good sauna with building methods other than cordwood masonry. People have used logs, silos, scrap lumber, all successfully. The original saunas may have been earthen. But a cordwood masonry sauna offers some distinct advantages—what I call the "Five E" advantages of cordwood.

ENERGY EFFICIENCY. A cordwood masonry wall offers a unique combination of insulation and thermal mass. The thermal mass of the inner mortar joint is separated from that of the outer mortar joint by an insulated space, so that its stored heat radiates back into the sauna more readily than to the outside air. The logs themselves also store heat and insulate.

ECONOMY. Cordwood masonry makes use of wood that might not be suitable for other styles of building. If a log or tree branch is curved even slightly, it is not much use as a post or to take to the sawmill for lumber. Cut into 9-inch pieces, however, the curvature is unnoticeable. Fire and disease-killed wood, old cedar fence rails and posts, recycled (untreated!) utility poles, even bits of scrap dimensional lumber, can all be made into good log-end material.

EASE OF CONSTRUCTION. Beavers, children, and grandmothers can (and do) all build cordwood buildings. (The beaver's home stays snug and sound through our long North Country winters, the "stove" being their own body heat.) If you can stack wood and make mud pies, you can build a cordwood wall. (Being able to frost a cake is a useful, too, but not absolutely necessary.)

ENVIRONMENTAL HARMONY. The cordwood sauna makes use of indigenous materials, not manufactured products, and even the leftover construction materials — scraps of wood, rejected log-ends — are used to heat the first two or three baths. And when the building finally gives up its ghost (which will be long after you give up yours), the materials will recede gracefully back into the landscape from which they came.

ESTHETICS. The Finns consider the sauna to be a spiritual place, like a church. So, as in a church, attention should be given to incorporating pleasing and artistic features into the design and construction. Cordwood masonry is a rustic style of construction. The warmth and texture of the wood contributes to the desired atmosphere. While sitting on a bench at 160 degrees or more, it is nice to be in pleasing or inspiring surroundings, not facing stark or bland walls. Building with cordwood is much like sculpting. Opportunities abound at both the design stage and during construction to include all kinds of special artistic features into the sauna — so many, in fact, that I am devoting the whole of chapter six to these esthetic considerations.

There you have it. These five reasons are why I call this joining of the sauna and cordwood masonry "a marriage made in Valhalla." If the gods aren't taking a cordwood sauna, they should be.

SITING

Before getting into cordwood construction techniques, we had better first ponder siting considerations, not the least of which is the irritating little question, "Do you have (or do you require, or can you get) regulatory permission to build your sauna?" Out in the country, this may not seem to be much of a problem, but, believe me, it can be. In

New York's Adirondack Park, for example, the sauna may be considered to be a building as defined under the strict zoning regulations enforced by the Adirondack Park Agency. This will be a consideration for me if I want to build a sauna on the edge of our lot on a nearby Adirondack lake. Setback from the lake will be another issue. While this all sounds like a pain, it is far less painful to secure the necessary permits prior to construction than to be hit with a removal notice later on.

Ask your local town building or zoning code enforcement officer about any necessary permits. In some localities, a permit may be required for any building; in others, a permit may be required only if the intended building will be greater than 100 square feet. Our round sauna, to give you an idea, is about 80 square feet, but the rectilinear one with the dressing room is about 150 square feet.

In Finland, saunas were built whenever possible next to lakes, rivers, or the Baltic Sea, because the Finns are great advocates of frequent cooldowns as a part of their baths. In rural North America there are also many sites that can take advantage of natural bathing nearby, although Americans may not be quite as enlightened as Finns are about neighbors running naked into the lake. So, while the lake or river site may seem perfect, some thought should be given to privacy.

There is a difference between privacy and being remote, however. The sauna must be sited near enough to home to be used. Particularly in winter, a really remote sauna will not be used as often as one sited more conveniently. In winter, paths have to be maintained and stove wood has to be hauled. A more remote site may have a special charm for a year or two, but, eventually, the romance wears thin. It's hard to set a fast rule on this, but I suspect that after 100 feet or so, a sauna's use will decrease in a linear proportion to the additional distance from the house.

On suburban lots, a privacy hedge or fence may be desirable. A swimming pool next to the sauna is a great plus: lucky you if you have one. If you don't, consider incorporating some sort of cooling tub as part of your sauna plan. It could be an old clawfoot tub, cattle trough, small children's pool, even an old oak whiskey barrel. A hot tub or spa doesn't offer that same tingling experience that is so valued by sauna enthusiasts, unless, of course, the heat is turned off.

If the site is hilly, or perhaps on a sloping shore, consider building on posts made of pressure-treated landscaping timbers, old rail ties, or even concrete pillars cast in heavy cardboard Sonatubes, which are peeled away from the concrete cylinders after 48 hours. Cordwood houses have been built on pillars, so a sauna is certainly possible. The main departure from the plans in this book would be the need for a few steps and the use of a wooden floor instead of the poured floors described.

The reader should be advised that all sorts of complications can come into play on a sloped site: erosion of the slope, safety issues, and just plain more difficult construction, to name a few. The sauna will be easier to build, safer to use, and probably less expensive to construct if a relatively flat, well-drained site is chosen.

Other siting tips: In the country, use natural foliage for privacy. As saunas are most often used in the afternoon, a westerly or southerly orientation is best. Consider any available view and how it might be integrated with sauna windows. Most importantly, don't rush into the project. Clearing the site, cutting trees, or any other environmental impacts should wait until you have a clear idea of the overall plan. And the plan, of course, should minimize environmental impacts.

HOW TO BUILD A CORDWOOD WALL

Now that you know where you want to build your cordwood sauna, it is time to learn how.

Choice of Wood

First, you'll need . . . cordwood! What kind? I like fellow cordwood addict Jack Henstridge's stock answer: Use what you've got. There is no point going to great trouble and expense to bring in some exotic wood if you have a perfectly acceptable alternative right on site. Like the beaver, use indigenous materials for environmental harmony.

Now, the answer to that simple question—What kind of wood?— might need refinement if you have a choice of species on your property. With any cordwood project, but particularly with a sauna, which is subject to great heat and humidity, I encourage the use of the lighter, fluffier woods, as opposed to the heavy, dense hardwoods. These lighter woods have a better insulation value and, more important, they have a lower coefficient of shrinkage and, therefore, expansion. They are more stable in the wall.

The terms hardwood and softwood can be deceiving. In general, hardwoods are deciduous, meaning they lose their leaves in winter, while softwoods are coniferous, or evergreen. Some hardwoods, such as poplar (quaking aspen), can be quite light when dry, while some softwoods, such as southern yellow pine, can be quite dense and hard. So, while softwoods are generally preferable to hardwoods for cordwood masonry, keep in mind the overlap of characteristics between these large groups.

The characteristic to look for is a low shrinkage. This is even more important than rot resistance. If you pay attention to the four rules already cited (use a good overhang, keep the wood off the ground, debark the wood, and use sound wood), you shouldn't have a problem with rot.

All the cordwood saunas I have built have been of Northern white cedar, which has about the lowest shrinkage characteristic you will find. It also has great rot resistance, excellent insulation value, an attractive yellow appearance, and a pleasant aroma. If Northern white cedar is on your list of available woods, seek no further.

Almost equally desirable would be: Alaska cedar, Atlantic white cedar, eastern (or western) red cedar, balsam fir, subalpine fir, white fir, eastern white pine, sugar pine, or redwood. For environmental reasons, I would shy away from the redwood unless it's recycled or dead. Incidentally, incense cedar might seem like a good choice because of its fragrance. It is not. I heard of one lady who complained that her sauna "stunk." The builder had used aromatic cedar boards for the walls. The "fragrance" was too much.

The next most desirable grouping would include bald cypress, bigtooth aspen, quaking aspen (poplar or "popple" in the northeast), butternut, sassafras, bigleaf maple, silver maple, blue ash, pumpkin ash, Douglas fir, Ponderosa pine, jack pine, red pine, tamarack (larch), or any spruce.

In a pinch, you might try Virginia pine, western white pine, or American chestnut.

Avoid dense hardwoods, such as any of the oaks, hickories, magnolias, birches, elms, maples not listed above, sweet gum, or sycamore, as well as the "softwoods" western larch, hemlock, or longleaf pine. In a house you could attend to the high shrinkage of these woods by applying a log chinking material to the mortar joints, such as Log Jam (by Sashco) or Perma Chink. But I don't know how well such flexible caulking materials will hold up at 200 degrees Farenheit. It seems safer to use a wood with low to moderate shrinkage characteristics.

Wood that can take on too much moisture can literally break a house apart. When wood wants to swell, nothing can resist it. Back in the old days, when explosives were expensive and labor was cheap, blocks of granite were broken off quarry faces by filling drilled holes with dry hardwood pegs and then wetting the pegs down. A series of expanding hardwood pegs would break off an 18-inch block of granite. Relatively weak mortar has no chance against this kind of hydrostatic pressure.

I don't mean to scare you with this, but I once had to tear walls down because of cordwood expansion. In 1980, I built part of the Earthwood home with mixed hardwood log-ends, split and dried a couple of years. All of my experience up until then had been with the benign white cedar. The dry hardwood swelled and broke up a beautiful wall. You don't have to repeat my mistake.

Seasoning the Wood

Having decided on a species of wood, the next question is: How long should the wood be dried prior to construction? The answer depends on the species.

In general, you want to give the less stable species less drying time, lest they dry so much they become "thirsty" and prone to expansion. Thus the preferred woods, those on the first list in the previous section, can be dried at their log-end length as long as you can afford to, up to a point of diminishing returns that occurs after about a year. As you work your way down through the preference lists above, less drying is recommended to counteract the potential of wood expansion, until, with the least preferred woods, only six to eight weeks of drying is recommended. Characteristics of wood, even within a species, may vary because of local climatic conditions. Wood is organic, not static. Remember that as you work your way down through the lists, greater wood shrinkage will occur. And, while wood shrinkage is not a structural problem, in the way that wood expansion is, it's not a particularly desirable characteristic in a sauna . . . or a home, for that matter.

Finally—because I want to instill reasonable caution without making too big a deal about this—if you're in doubt about the wood you have available, the best course of action is to test a small sample panel and see how it performs. Build a 2-foot high by 4-foot section of cordwood masonry wall with the wood you want to test. (You get valuable building practice, too, as a side benefit.) Wait ten days. Spray one side of the panel with water. After another 48 hours, examine the wall. If large cracks form between the log-ends on the side that was soaked, while only hairline cracks appear on the other side, the wood has probably swelled.

How Many Cords?

How much cordwood to prepare is a more exact science. The relevant unit to deal in is, of course, the cord! A true cord is a stack of wood four feet high, four feet wide, and eight feet long, or 128 cubic feet of wood. Commonly, though, wood is sold in *face cords*, also called ranks, ricks, or runs. A face cord is also a stack of wood four feet high and eight feet long, but its width is whatever length the logs were cut—12 inches, 16 inches, or whatever. Some wood merchants may be selling wood by the "cord" when they really mean the face cord. Mind the quality, and check the width.

Face cords are handy for our purposes, however. With cordwood saunas, we'll be dealing with log-ends of any uniform length from 8 to 12 inches, depending on your preference. With respect to heat loss, the larger the stoveroom, the thicker the cordwood walls should be. With a round sauna, log-ends can't be too long on a tight diameter, or the outer mortar joints will be disproportionately wide. With a 10-foot on diameter building, 8-inch log-ends work well, while 9-inch thick walls are the limit. With a 12-foot on diameter sauna, 10-inch log-ends will work. With rectilinear shapes, 8-inch-thick walls are adequate for a small sauna, while up to 12-inch logs may be used to build a large communal sauna.

The steps I follow to figure cordwood quantity are:

1. Figure out the square footage of the cordwood masonry portion of the sauna wall. If the sauna is round, like the Earthwood sauna described in chapter four, multiply the interior circumference by the height of the building, and subtract for the door and windows, using the outside door and window frame dimensions. If the sauna is rectilinear in shape and the building has a heavy post-and-beam frame, like the Log End Sauna described in chapter three, you can add up all the individual rectilinear panels to get the square footage of the cordwood. Then subtract any doors or windows.

2. Divide the cordwood square footage by 32. This will give you the number of face cords you would need if you didn't use any mortar.

3. Make a final adjustment for mortar, which I call Roy's 15 percent constant. That is, you can take 15 percent off the previous figure, derived in step 2, and rest assured that the mortar will more than make up the shortfall. In fact, you should have

enough wood to reject any questionable or awkwardly mis-
shapen log-ends. If you are cutting a lot of questionable log-
ends, eliminate this 15 percent adjustment. Better to have too
many than too few. Remember, there is no waste, as reject
log-ends will be used to heat the sauna.

What constitutes a reject log-end? Any piece with active rot or insect activity. Any piece with huge gnarls or branch knobs, which get in
the way. Any piece with one end a lot bigger or a different shape than
the other. Any piece more than ½-inch out of tolerance for length. The
length of the log-end, remember, constitutes the width of the wall. If
the piece is more than a half inch short, save it for firewood. If more
than a half inch too long, trim it—carefully!

Let's do a quick cordwood calculation for the round Earthwood
sauna described in chapter four. On round buildings, calculations are
based on the interior diameter, because it's the inner surface of the wall
that must have the correct thickness of mortar joint maintained, about
an inch. On the outside surface, mortar joints will be slightly larger in
the lateral direction.

The inside diameter for the plan in chapter four is 9 feet, 6 inches.
The inner circumference is the inside diameter times pi (3.1416), which
rounds to 29.85 feet (9.5 × 3.1416). Multiplying by the mean height of
the cordwood walls (7 feet, 4 inches, or 7.33 feet) yields 218.80 square
feet (7.33 × 29.85). Subtracting 15.16 square feet for the door and door
frame and 7.64 square feet for the two window frames leaves us with
196 square feet of cordwood area. Dividing by 32 converts square feet
to face cords: 196/32 = 6.13 face cords. I reject poor log-ends when I
stack them for measure, so I'll make my 15 percent adjustment: 85 percent of 6.13 (or .85 × 6.13) = 5.2 face cords—so call it five and a bit.

There, that wasn't so bad, was it? Measure out cords by making a
frame out of scrap lumber, the inner dimensions of the frame measuring 4 by 8 feet. Or you can drive stakes into the ground 8 feet apart,
leaving 4 feet of the stakes sticking out of the ground. Fill this frame
five times—and a bit—and you've got your cordwood.

Log-end Preparation

Students always ask me if split wood or rounds work best. My reply is
to choose the style you prefer. I've built cordwood walls with all
rounds, all splits, and a mixture of the two. Maintain a consistency of
style and they all look good. You can dry wood faster if it's split, in case

that's an important consideration. It's a little easier to maintain a constant thickness of mortar joint between log-ends if you have a variety of splits available, making pointing (or "grouting") that much easier. Also, big rounds will tend to shrink more. On the other hand, the big log-ends make pleasing design features and get a lot of wall up in a hurry. Look at the pictures in this book and make up your own mind. Experiment.

An important part of log-end preparation is to bark the wood. (Or you can "debark" it—means the same thing, which is to remove the bark.) Otherwise, after a year or two, the wood has a tendency to shrink away from the bark, creating a cozy space in which powder post beetles, carpenter ants, wasps, and other uninvited guests will take up residence. Barking is easiest if you cut trees in the spring, when the sap is rising. Bark them as soon as they hit the ground. Delay a week or two, and an easy job becomes very much more difficult. Some good barking tools are a trowel, a hatchet, the leaf spring from a pick-up truck, a hoe which has had its blade straightened under heat, and a sharpened square-tipped spade.

Another often necessary log-end preparation task, particularly with cedar, is to scrape off the "hair" or bits of fiber that are left on the ends of the logs during the cutting process. These attached fibers get in the way of the pointing knife, adding frustration to an already time-consuming job. The best tool we've found for removing this hair is a Stanley Sureform scraper. I like the kind with the handle that fits in your fist and which is used by pulling the small (2-inch square) scrap-

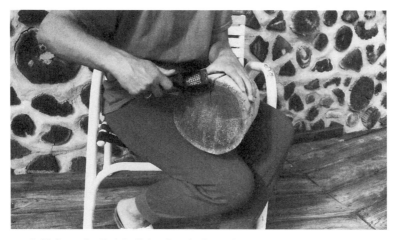

2-2. Jaki cleans the "hair" off the edge of a log-end.

ing blade toward you, quickly cutting the thin unwanted fibers. Once quickly around a round log-end does the job.

Estimating Other Materials

Besides log-ends, you will need sand, sawdust, lime, and Portland cement. While we've got the round Earthwood sauna example to follow, this would be a good time to discuss quantities.

SAND. For a sauna, a full-sized pickup truck load of masonry sand should do it. The sand should not be too coarse. If you have to choose between two piles, take a pinch of each and squeeze it between your thumb and forefinger, close to your ears. You want the quieter sand, not the noisy stuff. If you have a small pickup, fill it safely and see how far it goes. Maybe you will get away with that, maybe you will have to go back for a second load. As with all materials, this depends somewhat on the width of your walls and the thickness of your mortar joints.

PORTLAND CEMENT (TYPE 1 OR TYPE I). With 8 to 10-inch walls, a 90-pound (1 cubic foot) bag of Portland cement will take care of about 16 square feet of wall. In our example, the 196 square feet of cordwood masonry area divided by 16 equals about twelve bags. My advice is to buy less at first, maybe six or eight bags, and see how far it goes. Then you can more accurately figure how much more you will need to finish the job, basing your calculations on your actual experience to date.

LIME. You will use lime in the mortar mix and also as an admixture in the sawdust insulation. Use Type S lime, also called hydrated lime or builder's lime. Agricultural lime won't work. A 50-pound (1 cubic foot) bag will cover about 12 square feet of wall. Our 196 square feet of masonry divided by 12 requires about sixteen bags of lime. Again, buy eight or ten bags, and see how far it goes.

SAWDUST. You will use sawdust for insulation and as an admixture in the mortar. A pickup load will be more than enough. Get coarse softwood sawdust from a sawmill, not fine sawdust from a cabinetmaker's shop, and definitely not planer shavings. Avoid oak and other dense hardwood sawdust.

Many people are surprised to see sawdust listed among the ingredients for mortar. I've seen experienced masons cringe. "There shouldn't be any organic matter in yer mud, ya know!" Ordinarily, yes. But cordwood mortar must meet different demands from that used with brick, block, or stone. The problem is that the dry wood tends to pull moisture from the mortar very rapidly, causing rapid setting, and thus mortar shrinkage. The faster any cementitious material sets— plaster, concrete, mortar, whatever—the more it shrinks.

The sawdust solves this problem by introducing millions of little sponges into the mortar, each storing a tiny reservoir of water that will slow the drying. We have tried all sorts of schemes to retard the set of the mortar in an effort to reduce shrinkage. We have tried hanging plastic over the wall, even wet towels. On the whole, these efforts have been if anything counterproductive. Some builders have even sprayed the wall down with water—definitely not advised, as the water may cause wood swelling. The best way we have found to retard the set (for up to four days, incidentally) is with the soaked sawdust. The longer the set, the stronger the material, just as with concrete.

Tools for Cordwood Masonry Work

For mixing mortar, you will need: one industrial-sized wheelbarrow, either metal or plastic; two spades, one for dry goods, one for the wet sawdust; a hoe for mixing the ingredients; and buckets for water. For building a cordwood wall, you will need: rubber gloves; metal mortar pans; pointing knives (how to make your own inexpensively is described later); a 4-foot level; a Stanley Sureform scraper for cleaning the log-ends; a smaller hammer for helping to set awkward pieces; a large container for mixing the sawdust insulation with the lime; and a small bucket and tin can for pouring the insulation into place.

So much for the materials and tools; let's build. What, no foundation? Don't sweat it. (The sweat comes later.) For now, I just want to teach you to do the cordwood masonry. We will discuss different foundation techniques in subsequent chapters. In the meantime, you can practice your cordwood technique in the basement, on your driveway, or on a row of solid concrete blocks.

The Mortar

The first thing to learn is how to make proper cordwood mortar, called "mud" in the trade.

Arrange your materials (sand, sawdust, cement, lime) and tools (hoes, spades, buckets) in a handy semicircle around your mixing wheelbarrow. I like a good industrial grade wheelbarrow with a steel or heavy rubber body. Borrow such a barrow if you can find one in good shape. If your project is going to persist over several weekends, however, it is probably worth buying one. Try auctions or second-hand stores, but get a good one. Take care of your wheelbarrow by scrubbing it and rinsing it clean every night and it will last a lifetime. I bought two 5-cubic-foot steel-bodied barrows 16 years ago and use them often, and they still perform as well as new.

Caution: Wear rubber gloves throughout the mixing process. They protect your hands from getting scraped on the edge of the wheelbarrow, and from lime and cement getting into the cuts. More on this in a minute.

Next, mix the mortar. The magic cordwood mud recipe I use was developed and refined over a 5-year period of testing on various cordwood buildings. I have been using it successfully since 1980, and so have hundreds of other happy cordwood builders. The proportions given are equal parts by volume, not weight:

ROB ROY'S CORDWOOD MUD RECIPE

     9 parts masonry sand
     3 parts sawdust
     3 parts Type S lime
     2 parts Type 1 (or I) Portland cement

The day before you want to mix mortar, pass the sawdust through a ½-inch screen into a soaking vessel, such as an open-topped 55-gallon drum, and then soak all the sawdust thoroughly, at least overnight.

To prepare the mortar next day, add ingredients to the wheelbarrow using the following cadence:

     3 parts sand, 1 part sawdust, 1 part lime
     1 part Portland cement
     3 parts sand, 1 part sawdust, 1 part lime
     1 part Portland cement
     3 parts sand, 1 part sawdust, 1 part lime

Some fastidious cordwood builders have used small pails to measure out the ingredients with great precision. This assures great quality control, I admit, but I've never bothered. I just use equally rounded shovelfuls. Whether you decide on pails or shovels, I suggest that one be kept for the sawdust and sand (the wet stuff) and one for the lime and Portland (the dry goods.) The dry lime or Portland powders will start to cake on and stick to a wet shovel or pail.

If you use the cadence described above, the ingredients will almost mix themselves. But not quite. Work them over with a hoe until the mix obtains a consistency of color. (An inexpensive garden hoe works well. You don't need a heavy, expensive mason's hoe, the one with the two holes in the blade.) Next, slowly add water and continue working the mix with the hoe until it has the right consistency. And what is that? Well, if a one-inch thickness of mud is placed against the vertical side of the wheelbarrow, it should hold its shape and not slump away. If you make a 3-inch diameter snowball of the mud and toss it three feet in the air (one meter, in Canada), it should neither crumble when you catch it (too dry) or go "Sploot!" (too wet). I wish I could tell you an exact amount or proportion of water to use, but, alas, this depends on how wet your sand and your sawdust are. After a heavy rain (if my sand pile was uncovered), I have had times when we didn't need to add any water at all to the mix. The "dry" mix was the finished mix.

With a little practice and experience, you will get this mixing process down to about nine minutes. The mud will last the experienced builder about an hour, longer for neophytes.

Notice that I specify mixing in a wheelbarrow, not a gas or electric mixer. Some of our students are a little surprised by this, but I have my reasons. The mechanical mixer detracts from the peace and spriritual calm of the cordwood building site. It needs to be well-cleaned at lunchtime and again at the end of the day, or it develops incurable cancer of the diduberator. The "infernal frustration" engine must be kept going and maintained. I am sure that Murphy had cement mixers in mind when he developed his famous law. So, I don't want to bust your chops on this, but anyone who is building a sauna, of all things, ought to be mixing their mud by hand. You will have better quality control on the mud, too, because you are more closely involved with it. And, finally, to get the mud to the site, you need a what? A WHEELBARROW! So why not eliminate one step?

Laying Down the Mud

The mud is delivered to the site and you are ready to build wall. House walls of cordwood masonry are typically 16 to 24 inches thick in the North, 12 to 16 inches in the South, but sauna walls can be roughly half as thick. A good rule to follow with a cordwood sauna is to think of the wall width being like the French or Italian tricolor flags: divided into equal thirds. The colored ends of the tricolor correspond to the mortar joints, the white central portion of the flag corresponds to the sawdust-filled cavity. At cordwood workshops, I always supply students with a "cheat stick" to help them gauge this "equal thirds" pro-

2-3. The MIM stick.

portion. For a 9-inch wall, for example, I will make several 9-inch cheat sticks of 1 × 2 or similar scrap material, each divided by heavy black lines into three equal 3-inch segments. I even label them M for mortar, I for insulation (sawdust), and M again for mortar. So the stick says "M/I/M." These little gauges are easy to make and invaluable for helping students to check their mortar proportions. Any inexperienced builder should take a few minutes to make a little cheater or MIM stick.

Fellow cordwood builder Jack Henstridge taught me years ago that it is faster and easier to lay down mud with rubber gloves than with a trowel. Use mason's gloves or one of the many cloth-lined "heavy duty" household gloves available today. Unlined dish-washing or surgeon's gloves will wear out quickly, sweat like crazy, and are hard to get on and off quickly in case you want to scratch your nose or something. It is an absolute no-no to handle mortar with your bare hands. Within a day or two, nasty little "cement holes" will begin to form on your fingertips, and your hands will go through severe drying, cracking, and pain before they finally fall off your arms. You have been warned. I know: the gloves seem awfully cumbersome at first, and you have to develop some new hand muscles to grab the mortar easily (I go through this every spring), but tough it out for three days and you will get accustomed to them.

The wall-building process is simple. My son Rohan was teaching kids in Illinois to build cordwood walls before he was ten years old.

2-4. *On a 9-inch wall, lay down two beds of mortar, each 1 inch thick and 3 inches wide.*

Grab a handful of mud (if your hands are big; a double handful if they are small). Plunk it down on the foundation, right to the edge. Keep repeating, fast as you can, to create a long bed of mortar, perhaps four feet long for beginners. For a 9-inch wall, this outer bed will be about 3 inches wide. Keep it about an inch thick. Then, using your cheater or MIM stick as a guide, place another bed of mortar parallel to the first and with an appropriate empty space between. A double bed is thus created, with a 3-inch cavity between.

Shape the mortar bed with your thumbs. You want to create a roughly rectangular cross-section of mortar, about an inch thick and three inches wide. But don't be too fussy. Don't pat it and shape it and worry it incessantly. This only brings water to the surface and frustrates the mortar, whose goal in life is to set up hard. Plunk it down, shape it quickly, and leave it alone! You will make it beautiful during the pointing process.

Cordwood masonry takes time. Yet think of all the different things that you are doing when you lay down that log-end: You are creating structure, insulation, interior finish, exterior finish, and thermal mass (which is totally lacking with many other kinds of construction). A typical house might have nine or ten layers in the wall's cross-section to accomplish the same things.

We can also make the process less time-consuming by adopting certain efficiency strategies. Primary among these is: Handle one material at a time. First mud. Then insulation. Then wood.

Installing the Sawdust Insulation

The insulation can be almost any loose-fill type, though I would shy away from cellulose, particularly with a sauna, where the steam created might trap moisture. Vermiculite and perlite have been used successfully, but the most environmentally kind material is sawdust. It's a lot kinder to your wallet, too.

We treat the sawdust with lime, at a rate of about three small spadefuls of lime to an industrial-sized barrow-load of sawdust. The lime helps deter vermin and is also handy in case the wall gets wet for any reason, in which event the lime will actually set up with the sawdust and form a kind of rigid foam product inside the wall.

Work the sawdust and lime mixture with a hoe until a uniform whitish color is achieved. Screening the sawdust with a ½-inch screen is optional. If there is not too much bark and other foreign matter in it, don't bother. But if lots of flotsam and jetsam get in the way of pouring the sawdust easily into the 3-inch cavity, use the screen. (Always screen any sawdust that will be used as mortar admixture.)

The sawdust insulation is most easily poured into the cavity with a small bucket having a little built-in pour spout. Swing the bucket parallel to the wall, not perpendicular, which causes the sawdust to spill on the mortar. On a round building, pour the sawdust from the inside of the building, so that the natural arc of your swing corresponds to the curvature of the wall. Go with the flow. Literally.

In tight spots, like next to posts, a small can is very handy. Pinch the

2-5. Insulation is poured into the cavity with a small bucket.

open end slightly to make a pouring spout. Don't leave voids. But be careful: Too much sawdust can make it difficult to set the log-ends in place. The sawdust doesn't compress very well. Too much of it will spring the log-end out of its correct position.

Laying Up the Wood

Unless all your log-ends are the same size, you will want to get into a "random pattern" as soon as possible. If you lay down only 6-inch diameter pieces, for example, the wall will soon get into a pattern not unlike a honeycomb: a hexagonal configuration. It is a hard pattern to break, though, and you will soon run out of 6-inch log-ends. To avoid this, I deliberately choose a variety of sizes and shapes for the first course. After that, the wall seems to build itself. If the log-end has a long flat side, or if one axis of an oval piece is significantly longer than the other, I tend to keep the flat side down. This is simply good standard masonry practice, employed with stone masonry, too, to build a strong and stable wall.

Placing the log-end is easy. Just set it across the two mortar joints with a gentle back and forth sliding motion. Rarely is there a need to tap it into place with a hammer. You will feel a kind of suction bond if you try—gently—to lift the log-end out of the mud. Ultimately, there is no natural chemical bond between wood and mortar. The best we can hope for is a friction bond, where rough surfaces of the wood meet the mortar.

2-6. Set the log-ends with a gentle vibrating motion to create a suction bond.

Place the second log-end next to the first, with about a one-inch space between the pieces. This is the typical width of a cordwood masonry mortar joint. The width might be a little more or a little less than this. If too much smaller—a half-inch or less, for example—the wall will be hard to point, because the pointing knife won't fit between log-ends. The thinner mortar will also be more likely to crack.

On the other hand, if the space between logs is too great, say, three inches or more, you are mixing a lot more mud than is necessary, pointing will be very time-consuming, and the esthetics of the wall will suffer. After all, it is the wood—not the mortar—that provides the visual interest. The mortar, recessed in the background, provides the contrasting relief of the wall. We say that the wood is "proud" (or stands slightly in front) of the mortar background. This three-dimensional effect contributes to interesting patterns of light and shadow. The alternative—lack of relief—looks like cordwood wallpaper.

Cover the entire run of mortar with consecutive random-sized log-ends in this manner. Don't leave mortar uncovered, or it will stiffen and inhibit the setting of log-ends later on.

The Second Course

You will lay up the second course of masonry much as you did the first, except that now you will be following the hills and valleys created by the first course. This is the time to place extra mud between log-ends, as necessary. Remember the first rule of efficiency: Handle just one kind of material at a time. Sometimes, in tight quarters, you will have to keep shifting from mortar to sawdust to wood, but, in general, try to work in sections of three to six feet to gain economy of movement. After the mud is down, pour in the insulation. Jaki and I like to lightly tamp the sawdust between log-ends with our gloved fingers, to prevent any settling (and resulting voids) months or years later.

Selecting log-ends for the second and succeeding courses requires a bit more judgment than was needed for the first. People with a good sense of proportion will do well here. The technique I teach is to "take a mental picture" of the space that needs to be filled. Then I turn to my stock of wood and look for the angle or curvature that matches the mental picture. It's a bit like doing a jigsaw puzzle. An "inefficiency" that beginners often get caught up in is to look for the right log-end before the mortar has been placed. This is getting ahead of the job and usually wastes time, because the size and the shape of the space changes after you place the mortar.

2-7. The mud and sawdust of the second course follow the hills and valleys of the first course.

Sometimes two or more different log-ends will go in a certain space. In this case, I will step back and look at the wall as a whole to see if a large or small piece is more in demand. Have I been using too many of one size of log in an area? Given a choice, take the opportunity to get back to that random rubble look.

Incidentally, what I call the random rubble look is not merely an esthetic consideration; it also depletes the various sizes of logs at a steady rate, which helps maintain a consistency of style throughout the project. My view is that cordwood masonry looks good either in a pattern—such as the hexagonal configuration already mentioned—or in a consistent non-pattern. What looks bad is when an intended pattern cannot be maintained, or when the random rubble appearance takes on an unwanted pattern.

Jaki and I have another rule of selection that has served us well over the years: Always use the biggest log-end that will fit in a gap, as long as the minimal thickness of mortar joint is maintained. If the first log you choose wobbles about in the space, try one a little bigger. See here (with apologies to Goldilocks):

 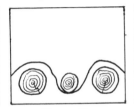 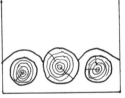

2-8.   *Too big!*   *Too small!*   *Just right!*

Really large log-ends may require some planning. Large natural "cradles" for such logs may not suddenly manifest themselves in the wall, particularly if you want to display a particular favorite piece in a certain place. Sometimes you must create the cradle. This takes some thought, but gets easier with experience. Fortunately, you will get your initial practice down low on the wall, where errors of proportion or mortar width will not receive much scrutiny.

With the rubble style of wall, another "rule" that will smooth progress is this: Always fill the valleys. By "valley," I mean the lowest spots along a section of cordwood. Never try to build on the high spots, the "hills." If you put mud on a hill, the chances are that it will stiffen before you can safely cover it with a log-end. A single log-end on top of another is prone to being knocked loose from its perch. When you fill the valleys, they will become the new hills, creating new valleys to fill. This is part of that phenomenon I refer to as "the wall building itself." When the work really flows, it is a wonderful experience. And creativity does not suffer, as you might expect. When you are really in tune, you become one with the wall, you do beautiful things together, and the sun is setting before you know it. It's magic.

Pointing

Mortar, sawdust, wood. Mortar, sawdust, wood. You can really get a rhythm going. Too bad production has to be slowed down by pointing. Also called "grouting," "raking," or "tuck pointing," pointing is the process of smoothing the mortar with a steel tool. There are special pointing tools made for block and brick work, but for rubble stone and cordwood masonry, a homemade pointing knife works best. We buy inexpensive butter knives at garage sales or thrift shops, and turn them into wonderful pointing tools by bending the last one-half inch of their blades to a 30-degree angle. And some owner-builders have been very happy using different sizes of stainless steel spoons.

Pointing serves several purposes. The obvious one is that it beautifies the wall. Let's say two walls are built side by side. One is laid up with a good sense of proportion, constant mortar joints, and a pleasing selection and variety of log-ends. But it doesn't get pointed. The other is poorly built: large sections of mortar, wood protruding too far from the wall, log-ends occasionally touching each other. But Jaki, our resident pointing artist, goes over the wall with her magic knife. Ten out of ten critics will select Jaki's wall as the better of the two.

There are other reasons besides appearance to point the wall. The bond between wood and mortar is maximized by tight, firm, tuck pointing. You will be surprised at how much pressure you can apply with your knife without pushing the mud into the sawdust cavity. This pressures tightens and strengthens the wall.

A pointed wall is also easier to keep clean. Cobwebs and dust balls find it harder to get a foothold.

Finally, pointing presents a water-repelling surface to the elements. A driving rain is much less likely to penetrate a smooth, well-pointed wall than a rough-textured mortar surface.

The pointing process has two steps: rough pointing, then finish pointing. The rough pointing consists of carving away excess (protruding) mortar, catching it in your gloved hand, and pasting it back into any obvious voids. We call this borrowing from Peter to pay Paul; and it may be poor economics, but it's an effective building technique. Rough pointing also gives us a chance to make sure that we have the right amount of mortar on the wall. Jaki and I like the appearance of log-ends being about one-quarter to one-half inch "proud" of the wall. Besides esthetics, there is a practical reason to take this approach: If, for any reason—wood shrinkage, mortar shrinkage, whatever—it becomes necessary to rechink the wall, the recessed mortar joint makes this possible. You would have little recourse with a flush-pointed wall.

Here I must interject a caveat. If your sauna plan calls for you to lean your naked body against the wall, you might prefer the cordwood

2-9. Jaki points a cordwood panel with an adapted butter knife.

wallpaper effect to the individual log-ends sticking you in the back. Our cordwood saunas all have maintained the textured relief that we find pleasing, and sometimes we have to adjust our position slightly to get comfortable, but it's not a problem. Alternatively, you can flush-point just where the wall will serve as a backrest, or you can install horizontal or vertical strips to the cordwood surface to create backrests.

Complete the rough pointing on a modest section of masonry before doing the finish pointing, lest you find that the mortar has gone too stiff to point. Finish pointing is easier to do on mortar that is somewhat set, as you are not trying to displace the stuff; you are merely putting a smooth finish on it. Some people just do the rough pointing and leave it at that. This wall still looks infinitely better than with no pointing at all, and takes much less time to build than one you finish point as well. (Some people simply point the wall with their rubber gloves, no tool at all. This is quick and easy, but leaves a much rougher texture in the mortar—though if done consistently throughout the building, it doesn't look bad.) Make your decision after you find out how you like pointing (some people, usually men, hate it) and how quickly you can reach your fussiness quotient.

Jaki is queen of the finish pointers. She works the mortar so smooth that you can hardly find evidence of the knife anywhere in the wall. It looks great (other cordwood builders have marvelled at the work) but it takes time and practice. And she is careful not to overwork the mor-

2-10. *Cordwood expert Cliff Shockey uses heavy rubber gloves to achieve a flush-pointed appearance. Later, log-ends are cleaned with a wire brush.*

tar. Constant smoothing with the knife can actually draw too much water to the surface and cause mortar shrinkage.

Speed increases with practice, so don't settle for a low standard of quality too early in the project. Remember the one and only Universal Truth: Everybody's different. You've got to find your own level of satisfaction. Keep a consistency of quality (rough or glove pointing should be considered the minimum standard) and the masonry will look great.

Finishing Up for the Day

All the mud is gone, you've got the pointing to your desired standard of quality, and you would dearly like to just stand back with a beer in hand and admire your work. Not so fast. There are a few necessary chores.

First and foremost, clean up your wheelbarrow, your tools, and any mortar trays or pans that used during construction. This is very important. Once steel tools start to build up a little hard mortar, they just keep getting worse until you are reduced to grinding them clean or (shudder) bashing them with a hammer. I scrub my wheelbarrows with a stiff-bristled plastic utility brush, being especially careful to get into the corners. Then I stand the barrow up and splash it with a bucket of clean water.

Clean up any spilled mortar off the foundation. A hoe, flat trowel, scraper, even a dustpan, are all useful tools for this job.

Cover the tops of your unfinished cordwood walls to protect them from rain penetrating into the insulation cavity. I use 6-mil plastic weighted down with blocks, stones, or log-ends, but any waterproof cover will work. Also, cover the bags of Portland cement and lime, and either keep the bags off the ground on a wooden pallet or bring them inside.

Make sure you have enough soaked sawdust for the next day's mortar. Set the ½-inch screen over the soaking vessel and shake the sawdust through into the water, discarding the chaff into a pile. The stuff you catch in the screen makes good landscaping mulch. Add enough water to cover the sawdust.

Rinse the rubber gloves, keeping the cloth lining dry. If you are good about this, one pair will last the whole project.

Now, admire your work. It looks a lot better when the chores are done. And the beer tastes better.

· 3 ·

The Post-and-Beam
Log End Sauna

THE POST-AND-BEAM log-end sauna can be a great sauna. We used it for years, and it is still in use today. The design incorporates a useful antechamber, which can serve as both a changing and relaxation room. The plan and construction is elegantly simple. If you have never built anything before, this project is approachable, even if you need to break down and ask your brother-in-law's help to set up the heavy frame. And why such a heavy frame? This sauna, like some others in the book, features a heavy earth roof.

The support structure consists of just six posts, three girders, and six roof joists: fifteen heavy timbers. That's it. Even if it takes two days to connect these fifteen timbers, so what? You're ready for the planking and the roofing. Soon the building is covered, and cordwood masonry can commence. Windows, doors, benches, stove and stovepipe—voila, you're ready to sweat.

Well, maybe not quite that fast. But construction follows small, logical steps. As with any building project, this one starts at the ground.

THE FLOATING SLAB FOUNDATION

The simplest foundation is the "floating slab," and it is my favorite with cordwood masonry because of its ease of construction, economy, and frost resistance. (The floating slab was Frank Lloyd Wright's

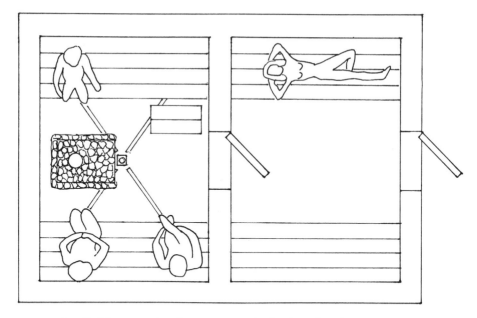

3-1. Log End Sauna consists of a stoveroom and a dressing/relaxation room.

favorite foundation system, too. It is said that great minds think alike. A Scottish friend, unfortunately, reminds me, "Aye, and fools seldom differ." But old Frank was no fool.)

In its pure form, the floating slab consists of a single, monolithic (meaning cast in a single pour), reinforced concrete slab that "floats" on a subfoundation (or "pad") of good percolating material such as coarse sand, gravel, or crushed stone. Typically, the slab has a thickened edge footing under the external walls. This is the way all of our round outbuildings at Earthwood are founded, as well as Mushwood, our cottage at the lake (so-named because of its resemblance to a mushroom). This is also the way we founded our latest version of this rectilinear sauna building, the Guest House at Earthwood, which appears in many of the illustrations in this book.

To understand how the floating slab offers protection against frost damage, it is important to know what causes "frost heaving" in the first place. When water freezes, it expands some 4 percent, and there is nothing you can do to stop it. Just as a jar of water left outside in the winter will freeze and break, or a cast-iron engine block unprotected by anti-freeze will crack and roads and sidewalks buckle, even a five-story building will heave if wet earth beneath the foundation freezes.

The common approach to avoid this problem is to take the foundation to a depth that is "frost free." In northern New York, the frost-free depth is considered to be four feet (48 inches). Building regulations in the city of Plattsburgh require that any new structure, even new front steps, be founded to a depth of 48 inches. This approach usually works, until that odd year when there is no insulating snow before severe cold sets in, a freak rain occurs, and a frost depth of 60 inches shifts the building.

The floating slab approach does not try to outguess the frost depth. It goes straight to the heart of the problem: it percolates the water away from the vicinity of the slab. No water, no frost. No frost, no heaving. No heaving, no problem.

To see how to create a floating slab, I will use the original Log End Sauna as an example, with some supplementary pictures taken during the Guest House construction.

First, remove all the organic material (topsoil, grass, weeds, etc.) to the edge of the site. You can do this with a bulldozer or a pick and shovel. A good powered tiller can help by loosening the soil, saving a lot of work if a dozer is not readily available. Stockpile this valuable organic material—"black gold"—at the edge of the site, ready for use later on the earth roof.

Next, we build up a "pad" of good coarse sand, gravel, or crushed stone. These materials have excellent "percolation characteristics," which means they don't hold water very well. At Log End Sauna, we chose sand for our pad, and we compacted it in layers, or "runs," of about 5 to 6 inches deep. Compacting layers more than 6 inches deep is difficult, even with the best powered compactor. At the Earthwood Guest House recently (a sauna by any other name) son Rohan and I compacted the sand by hand with 8-inch concrete corner blocks. We kept our runs about 3 to 4 inches deep and, yes, it was hard work. Whether you compact by hand, or hire a compactor, wet the sand down to get decent compaction. Pounding dry sand is an exercise in futility. Now I know why, when I was a little kid and being a pest, my father would tell me to go pound sand.

For a small building like the sauna, the pad can be built up about 8 inches higher than surrounding grade. Then the concrete slab is "floated" on this pad. One caution: If in scraping off the organic material you have exposed nonpercolating clays, hardpan, shale, or other earth that won't drain, you will need to incorporate a drain in the pad itself, such as 4-inch perforated drain "tile" or hose. This drain will remove any water that might collect in the pad and carry it to some point downgrade. Now there will be no frozen lens of water to form under

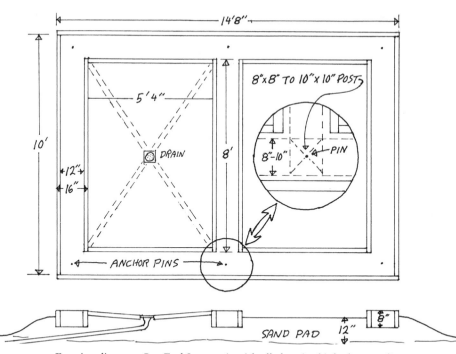

3-2. *Forming diagram, Log End Sauna. As with all plans in this book, exact dimensions can be adjusted somewhat to make use of available materials. Do not diminish any dimensions having to do with supporting an earth roof. Forming boards are 2 x 8-inch planks, well-staked (say, every 4 feet or so). The diagram assumes full dimensional (rough-cut) material. The drain and sawdust floor sections can be done later, but they are shown here for convenience.*

the building. If such a drain is needed, it can double as the washwater drain, described later.

I always extend the pad to include a sloping skirt to support the extremities of the slab. Later, when the building is completed, I cover the skirt with 6-mil black polyethylene (also called Visquene) and, finally, with 2 inches of #2 crushed stone. The plastic and crushed stone prevents any roof runoff from eroding the pad and keeps grass and weeds from growing close to the cordwood walls. The width of the skirt is typically 30 to 36 inches.

Preparing for the Foundation Pour

We made a slight modification to the classic floating slab design at the Log End Sauna, but the preliminary work was the same: Scrape the organic material to the edge and built up a pad of compacted sand. As

3-3. Topsoil is scraped to the edge of the site and a pad of sand has been built up. The 2 x 8 form boards are in place. The "floating ring beam" is ready to pour.

the photo and drawing reveal, we cast a "ring beam" instead of a slab. The ring beam is just a fancy term for a continuous rectilinear footing around the perimeter of the building, with another internal footing (sometimes called a "grade beam") where the dividing wall between stove room and antechamber is located.

For a sauna, a standard concrete slab floor can be rather cold on the feet. This problem can be eliminated by the use of "duckboards," something like pallets, for standing on. These duckboards are common in commercial saunas, and even in Finnish saunas in the old country. But the duckboards have to be kept clean and dry, which is a maintenance situation I would just as soon avoid. Our solution is the "sawdust concrete" floor, described later.

Our footing forms were made of 2 × 8 stock, at the dimensions in figure 3-2. I bought new boards for the purpose, because I had in mind to use them again and again, but sometimes you can borrow forming boards from a contractor friend. Another plan is to use four of the roof rafters that you are going to need later on, as the outer forming boards. Just leave them extending past each corner.

As our walls were to be 8 inches wide, I decided on 12-inch wide footings, to lessen the load on the sand pad. With a sand pad, it is easy to make a 4-inch deep track in the pad where the footing forms are to be placed. I use a hoe and shovel to draw this track, and I place the excavated sand just outside the footing forms, on the skirt area, for use in helping to resist concrete "blow-out" during the pour. After the forms are removed, this sand is simply raked out onto the skirt area.

While it is still easy to work in the sand pad, install the stove room drain, which will carry washwater away. Two-inch diameter Schedule 40 ABS or PVC pipe is easy to work with. At the center of the stove room, a floor drain, like a shower drain, is installed so that its top surface is one inch below the top of the foundation (footing forms). The drain is connected with a 90-degree elbow to a length of 2-inch Schedule 40 pipe of sufficient length to carry washwater out above grade or to a soakaway (greywater) pit. This drain pipe will need to go under the footing, so it is most easily installed now.

If the sauna is located on a large wooded country lot, I would just run the pipe out above grade. We are only dealing with a few gallons of relatively clean water here. But check with local codes. A greywater soakaway pit may be required.

In any case, you must maintain a pitch of 2 inches of drop for every 10 feet of pipe. Make sure that the sand is dampened and firmly tamped all around the pipe, so that it doesn't settle later on. Also, make sure the drain and first short vertical section of the drain pipe are glued and firmly staked, perhaps to a short piece of ½-inch reinforcing rod driven into the sand pad. Carefully tape the top surface of the drain to keep sand from falling in.

Prior to setting the form boards in their tracks, cover almost all of the sand pad with a 13 by 17-foot sheet of 6-mil black polyethylene. The plastic will conform to the shape of the footing tracks just created. Its purpose is fourfold: (1) It prevents the sand from robbing the moisture from the concrete too quickly, which would cause rapid setting and weaken the concrete. (2) If the plastic is wrapped over the inner surface of the outer footing forms, the boards will be easy to remove after the concrete has cured, and they will be nice and clean, particularly important if they are to be used later as rafters. (3) After the forms are removed, the exposed plastic at the edge of the building can be folded or rolled up close to the foundation, available for use later on when the skirt is covered with additional plastic and crushed stone. (4) Later, when the sawdust concrete floor is poured, the plastic will serve again in retarding the rapid setting of the pour. If you don't use this plastic, be prepared to work awfully fast. And be sure to oil the forming boards for ease of removal later on.

Footing form boards can be fastened to each other with ordinary 16-penny (16d) nails, but I prefer buying a few 16d forming nails, which are double-headed. These nails are also called "duplex," "double-headed," or "scaffolding" nails. They are driven in to the first head only. Later, removal is easy because you can get the claw of your hammer (or a crow bar) under the second head. Check the footing

3-4. Six-mil plastic covers the entire slab at the Guest House. Rebar is placed in the footing track and 6 × 6 × 10 × 10 wire mesh is placed in the floor area. Son Rohan applies Acryl-60 bonding agent to the underside of roofing slates, which are set into the concrete while it was still plastic. See pages 69-71.

forms for level and square. Square is easily checked by measuring along the diagonals. If the two diagonal measurements are the same, the building is square. If they are not, make adjustments until they are. Oil the small "inner circle" forming boards for ease of removal later on.

Some books and articles recommend the use of "batter boards" for use in getting the foundation square. I have found them to be more trouble than they are worth. Just use your tape measure and four wooden stakes to get the pad and rough layout of the footing tracks in the right place. Keep checking those diagonals. This whole trial and error process will take about 15 minutes with two people and a tape measure; the batter board method takes a lot longer.

And speaking of stakes, use plenty of well-driven wooden 2 × 2 or 2 × 4 stakes around both the inner and outer perimeters of the forming boards. A stake every four feet is a good guide. These stakes will prevent concrete blow-out, particularly with ready-mix concrete.

With a building that is to be kept permanently heated, I would advise placing extruded polystyrene at both the outside edge and at the bottom of the footing track. With a sauna, which is only heated for a few hours (and where floor level temperature is not too important) there is economy in leaving out the footing (or slab) insulation.

Place two continuous pieces of ½-inch reinforcing bar ("rebar") in the footing track, each about 3 inches in from the edge of the footing forms and about 3 inches off the bottom of the footing track. Support the rebar with 3-inch thick pieces of clean broken brick or clean flat stones, either of which will become a part of the footing itself. As rebar comes in 10- or 20-foot lengths, it will be necessary to overlap pieces (a 20-inch lap is the code requirement) and wire them together with forming wire. Bend the rebar to go around corners.

Pouring the Footings

As drawn, the footings require about 1¼ cubic yards of concrete. (Here is the math for those who wish to make alterations to the dimensions: The two long tracks are each 14 feet, 4 inches long. The three shorter tracks are each 8 feet long. All the tracks added together total 52 feet, 8 inches. At 1 foot long by 8 inches wide [.667 feet], each running foot of the foundation will hold .667 cubic feet of concrete [1 foot × 1 foot × .667 = .667 cubic feet]. Multiplying 52.667 running feet times .667 cubic feet per running foot yields 35.13 cubic feet of concrete required. Dividing cubic feet by 27 gives us the answer in cubic yards, 1.3 in this case, just over 1¼ cubic yards.)

Now you have two choices: Call for the ready-mix truck from the nearest concrete plant, or mix it yourself with a mixer or in a wheelbarrow. Economically, there really isn't much difference except for one little detail: The batch plant is going to charge a hefty "small load charge" for delivering such a small quantity of concrete. At the Earthwood Guest House, which required two cubic yards, it was worth my while to pay this small load charge, about $60, and I did. With 1¼ yards, you might consider mixing your own (for economy) or waiting until you—or a neighbor—need a few yards of concrete for another purpose. Just add the 1¼ cubic yards to the amount required for the other job.

If you decide to make your own concrete, you can mix the constituent ingredients in a barrow or mixer, or you can buy ready measured bags of dry concrete mix, such as Sakrete or others. Each bag of Sakrete provides .66 cubic foot (.66 CF), so you will need about 53 bags (53 × .66 = 34.98 cubic feet). You can mix two bags at a time in a barrow, so you are looking at repeating this exercise—and exercise is the operative word—about 27 times. You can see why I am a great fan of ready-mixed concrete.

A good recipe for making your own concrete from scratch is: 3 parts #1 crushed stone, 2 parts sand, 1 part Portland cement. You will need about 6 bags of Portland, and you'll still need to mix a couple of dozen batches in your wheelbarrow.

The concrete should be fairly stiff for maximum strength. Tell the concrete company that you want a 3-inch slump. You will impress them with your use of the inside terminology. *Slump* is how far a pile of concrete will collapse, or slump, when a standard metal cone is removed from a sample.

Pour the concrete into the tracks and screed it level to the top of the forms using a 24-inch piece of scrap 2 × 4 or similar material. Be sure to tamp the concrete into the corners of the footing tracks to eliminate air pockets. After the concrete is poured and screeded (in the case of ready-mix, this happens fast), you can trowel the stuff nice and smooth with a flat finishing or plasterer's trowel. If mixing your own, you might have to trowel after each 2 or 3 barrow loads so the concrete doesn't get too stiff to work.

While the concrete is still workable, install a 6-inch long anchor bolt at the exact center of each of the six "corners"; this includes the two intersections where the internal wall footing meets the long sides. The anchor bolts will anchor the base of the framing posts. The bolts are usually ⅜ or ½ inch in diameter and have one end threaded and the other end bent at a 90-degree angle. Stick the bent end into the concrete and leave about 1½ inches of the threaded end exposed. Trowel carefully in this area so the 8 × 8 posts have a good flat surface to rest upon later.

3-5. The author trowels the concrete soon after it is poured. Anchor bolts are set in the concrete as per figure 3-2.

Wash all your tools and you are done for the day.

Remove the forms two days after the last of the concrete has been poured. Clean the forms with a trowel, scaper, or wire brush, particularly if you have borrowed them or if the long ones are to be used as roof rafters.

THE POST-AND-BEAM FRAME

The simple frame consists of six posts made of 8 × 8-inch stock. Use old recycled barn beams, newly milled timbers, or members hewn from your own trees. In any case, the materials list is the same, and the dimensions work well; I have built this building three times. If you are really tall or prefer higher ceilings inside, you can add 4 inches to the post heights given.

You will need the following materials:

Posts (8" × 8")	Girders (8" × 8")	Rafters (2" × 8")
2 @ 5'8" (68")	3 @ 10'8" (128")	6 @ 16'0" (192")
2 @ 6'6" (78")		
2 @ 7'4" (88")		

Cut the post ends as square as you possibly can. If you do a better job squaring on one end than the other, put the good end down. With old barn timbers, make sure that they are still in good condition. Reject any with existing deterioration. Any used as girders must be perfect.

Prior to standing the six posts, I like to mark the exact locations of their 8-inch-square footprints on the foundation with a pencil or crayon. A tape measure and carpenter's square are the only other tools you need. At the original sauna, I kept the walls and posts 2 inches in from the edge of the footings. At the Guest House, I kept the posts just one inch in from the edge, and this is my recommendation to the reader. As the Guest House log-ends were actually 9 inches long, the cordwood walls are built almost out to the edge of the slab.

Next, cut six 8 × 8 squares of 240-pound asphalt shingle and place them over the footprints marked on the foundation. These asphalt squares act as a "damp-proof" course under the posts, stopping what the Brits call "rising damp" from entering the bottoms of the posts. This is very important. Bits of thick roll roofing or waterproofing membrane (such as the Bituthene you will use on the earth roof) also serve well. You will need to cut a little hole in the membrane for the anchor bolt.

On either side of the square footprint I place concrete blocks to serve as a guide for positioning the post, as in figure 3-7. Rohan holds the post in position, balanced on the positioning pin. When he nods his head, I hit it with the sledge hammer—the post, that is. That marks the location for the pin on the post's base. We take the post down and drill a hole into that mark, using a drill of the same diameter as the anchor pins. Drill a little deeper than the height the pin extends above the foundation. Now put the post back up. With the damp-proof course actually helping to stabilize the post (it compresses as needed, helping to compensate for any irregularities in the troweling) the post will usually stand quite happily by itself.

Next, plumb and crossbrace all six posts with scrap material. Only then should you attempt to place the three heavy girders. (Construction hint: With a pencil and square, lay out the location of the posts onto the underside of the girders prior to lifting them in place. Make sure that the spacing of your marks corresponds to the actual spacing of the posts on the foundation.) You can pin the girders to the posts if you like, or you can join them with truss plates. Or, as we did, you can install about four "toenails" or "toe screws" at a 45-degree angle up through the post into the girder. Put the nails or screws where they will be hidden by the cordwood masonry.

3-7. A good tap with a sledge hammer makes an impression of the anchor pin on the underside of the 8 × 8-inch post.

3-6. The damp-proof square covers the footprint where the 8-inch square posts are to be erected.

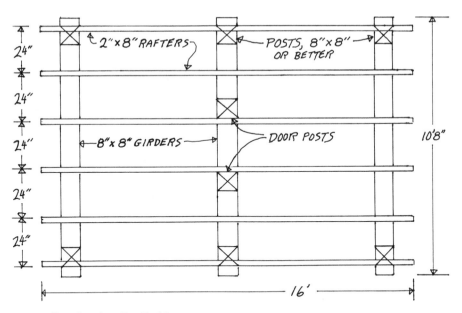

24″
24″
24″
24″
24″
24″

10′8″

2″x8″ RAFTERS

POSTS, 8″x8″ OR BETTER

DOOR POSTS

8″x8″ GIRDERS

16′

3-8. Framing plan, Log End Sauna.

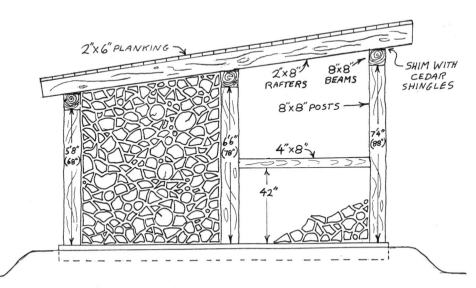

2″x6″ PLANKING

2″x8″ RAFTERS

8″x8″ BEAMS

8″x8″ POSTS

SHIM WITH CEDAR SHINGLES

74″ (88″)

5′8″ (68″)

6′6″ (78″)

4″x8″

42″

3-9. West elevation, Log End Sauna.

3-10. All six posts are plumbed, then braced to stakes with scrap lumber.

After the girders are temporarily (but firmly) crossbraced, the six 16-foot-long 2 × 8 rafters can be installed. Rather than "bird's mouthing" (cutting notches into) the rafters to stabilize them atop the girders, I prefer to shim under the rafters with little cedar shims made for the purpose, and available quite inexpensively at a building supply store.

The outside dimensions of the sauna walls are actually 10 feet by 14 feet, 4 inches, so 24-inch center-to-center spacing (known as 24-inch on-center) works well with either planking or plywood. The reason the girders are listed as 10 feet, 8 inches is so they can extend proud of the wall by 4 inches on each end. This looks good and makes it easier to fasten the rafters. For an earth roof, use at least ¾-inch CDX (exterior grade) plywood. Without the earth roof, ⅝-inch plywood would suffice.

Full-sized (rough cut) 2 × 8 rafters are recommended, particularly if an earth roof is to be supported. If they are unavailable, use nominal "two-by-tens," which are actually 1½ by 9¼ inches nowadays. The rough cut material, still available at country sawmills, is not only stronger, but much more in keeping with the rustic design of the building.

Erecting these fifteen load-bearing members is the toughest part of the whole project. Take your time. Get some help. Measure twice, cut once.

Roof Decking

The choices for roof decking are plywood or 2 × 6 planking. I have used recycled 2 × 6 spruce silo planking, recycled decking, and new 2 × 6 tongue-and-groove V-joint planking. The new stuff is the nicest looking, the easiest to work with and, obviously, the most expensive. The greater cost, though, could be offset by the diminished hassle.

I have never used plywood for the ceiling of a sauna. I believe the glues would hold up okay, but have no personal evidence to support this. If you are sensitive to the chemicals that go into making the glues, avoid it. Plywood will not look as nice as solid planking, either.

The planking should overhang the edge of the cordwood wall by 12 inches. Remember that the outer surface of the outermost rafters is in the same plane as the cordwood walls. With the 10-foot-wide building dimension shown in the plan, 12-foot planking will work perfectly. You won't need to make a single cut! If plywood is used, follow the spacing plan given below. Make sure that the plywood or planking overhangs the rafter ends by an inch or two at the front and back of the building. This may necessitate shortening the rafters just slightly, at which time I cut their leading edges to a true vertical, for appearance's sake as well as for drip protection.

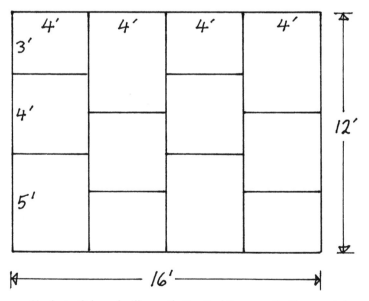

3-11. Six sheets of plywood will cover the Log End Sauna roof with no wasted material, if this cutting and placement diagram is used. All of the new cuts (the horizontal lines on the diagram) fall on the rafters, which are 24 inches on center. A 12-inch sidewall overhang is assumed.

THE EARTH ROOF

As designed, the roof of this sauna (like most) has a fairly shallow pitch, specifically 1½:12. These cryptic numbers mean that the roof pitch rises 1½ inch for every 12 inches of lateral run, which just happens to be the recommended pitch for an earth roof.

A properly built earth roof is the longest lasting roof you can build. The earth protects the roof surface from the two enemies that break down every other roofing material: the sun's ultraviolet rays and constant freeze-thaw cycling. In upstate New York, an ordinary roof may be subjected to as many as thirty freeze-thaw cycles in a winter, each one causing further microscopic deterioration.

The earth roof is also the only spiritually compatible roof for an outdoor sauna, helping the building blend with the natural world and returning the sauna to its roots of thousands of years ago, when the baths were built underground.

The steps for building an earth roof are:

1. **Drip Edge**. Install a drip edge all around the perimeter of the planked deck. Anodized aluminum or galvanized iron drip edge is available in 10-foot lengths at building supply yards; galvanized is the more economical choice. Typically, about 4 inches of the drip edge shows on the top roof surface, providing a good receiving surface for the waterproofing membrane.

2. **Waterproofing**. I have had good success over the years with W. R. Grace's Bituthene Waterproofing Membrane, now called System 4000. It consists of a top surface of two layers of cross-laminated black polyethylene over a 60-mil (1/16 inch) base of sticky rubberized asphalt. The rolls are three feet wide by 35 feet long, so they cover about a "square" (100 square feet). Two rolls will do the 192-square-foot sauna roof deck with practically no waste. A removable backing paper protects the sticky bitumastic until the moment of application.

    Before installing the membrane, roll a thin coating of the compatible primer onto the wooden deck. This primer is supplied by Grace as a part of the system. Allow the primer to dry, which takes less than an hour. Installation of the membrane is quick and easy with two people. One person rolls the Bituthene out onto the deck, lapping the drip edge by three inches, while the second person pulls the backing paper off the under-

3-12. The waterproofing membrane is applied to the roof deck.

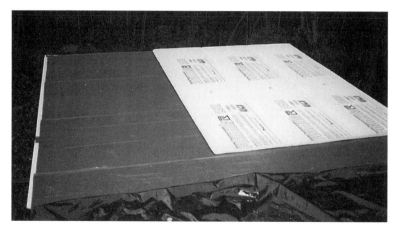

3-13. An inch of extruded polystyrene protects the membrane and supplies extra insulation. This rigid foam, in turn, is covered with 6-mil black polyethylene.

side of the roll. Use horizontal courses, beginning with the bottom course at the lower end of the roof, and then work your way up the roof with succeeding courses. Press the membrane firmly onto the deck, using the heels of your hands. The stuff really sticks, particularly if you use the compatible primer. Succeeding courses lap the first by 2½ inches, following a guide line stamped on both edges of the roll.

There are other methods of waterproofing, but it is outside the scope of this book to discuss the subject in great detail. I have waterproofed two saunas successfully with Bituthene and do not hesitate in recommending it as an easy-to-install and moderately priced waterproofing system. (See my earlier book, *The Complete Book of Underground Houses*, listed in the bibilography, for a more complete discussion of the earth roof.)

3. **Insulation**. To protect the membrane and add an extra R-5 of insulation to the roof, I cover the Bituthene with an inch of extruded polystyrene foam insulation such as Dow Styrofoam Blueboard or Grayboard, or UC Industries Foamular, a pink-colored foam board. Twelve 2 × 8-foot sheets cover the deck completely, with no cutting and no waste.

4. **Plastic**. Next, lay out a single piece sheet of 6-mil black poly-ethylene over the insulation board. This plastic sheet forms the base of an important drainage layer.

5. **Drainage Layer**. Over the plastic, install a 2-inch drainage layer of crushed stone, either #1 or #2 (roughly 1-inch stones). The combination of the inexpensive poly sheet with the stone drainage layer has the effect of taking most of the water to the edge of the building, greatly reducing pressure on the membrane. This is cheap insurance.

6. **Filtration Mat**. Next, place a 2- to 3-inch layer of loose hay or straw over the crushed stone. This layer serves as a natural organic filtration mat. It eventually decomposes and compresses to about ¼-inch thick, but it keeps on working, keeping the drainage layer clean.

7. **Sods or Retaining Timbers**. Around the edge of the roof, place moss or grass sods to retain the soil to follow. These sods should be about 6 inches wide, 12 inches long, and 5 to 6 inches thick. Cut them from a grassy or mossy area with a sod cutter or square-tipped spade. You will need about 55 to 60 of them if each is a foot long. (You could sod the whole roof in this way, as we did with our first underground house, but that is a lot of work.) I find these edge sods to be superior to retaining timbers for holding the earth on the roof. They also drain more naturally.

If you prefer railroad ties or 6 × 6-inch pressure-treated landscaping timbers, be sure to shim them up on pieces of 1 or 1½-inch pressure-treated wood, particularly the timbers

3-14. The earth roof at Log End Sauna.

along the low edge, to give the water an easy route off the roof. Otherwise an ice dam can occur, which could promote a leak. Good drainage is always the better part of waterproofing.

8. **Earth**. Install 7 to 8 inches of soil; this will eventually compact to about 6 inches. Plant it with all kinds of wildflowers and cover it with mulch. Some flowers will flourish; others won't make it. Eventually, just the right vegetation will be growing up there. Don't even think about mowing the roof. Wild is the look we're after. The only watering you might need to do will be during the first few weeks, until the sods get reestablished in their new home and the wildflowers start to bloom. I have never watered any of my earth-roofed saunas, and they are replete with vegetation and support their own little microecosystems.

How do you get all that crushed stone and earth up on the roof safely? Well, the best way is to construct a good solid set of wooden steps and just march right up there with a pail of earth balanced in each hand. By the end of the day, your wingspan will have gained four inches. Why not get help from all those friends that you're going to invite to share your sauna?

If you use pressure treated material for your steps, as we have done, they can be a permanent means of accessing the roof. In the summer, you might just like hanging out up there after a sauna. Just stay away

3-15. The principle design elements at Log End Sauna. Illustration by Sally Onopa.

from the edge, please. Safety here is your responsibility, not mine. Don't create an "attractive hazard" for local kids. Remove the steps when not in use.

I anticipate two objections to my earth roof dissertation. The first will be from nonbelievers. Somehow, they will have accepted both saunas and cordwood masonry, but the earth roof is just too much. Some have expressed a nervousness, almost a claustrophobia, knowing that there are tons of earth overhead. Of course, if you led them blindfolded into the sauna, then removed the blindfold, they would have no way of knowing that they were underground. But no matter. Their minds are like good concrete: all mixed up and fully set. To these people, I say, okay, I'm sorry I can't convince you. The other options for a shallow pitched roof are to install a good-quality half-lap roll roofing (10-year life expectancy) or a more expensive chemically- or heat-bonded "modified" roof, which will last about 25 years. Remember that you will need to incorporate some kind of insulation (at least R-10) into the roof system. You cannot just leave the waterproofing membrane exposed to the ultraviolet rays of the sun; it will begin to deteriorate within a year. Protected, it will last a lifetime.

The other objection I anticipate is one that pops up frequently at our building school, and I'm actually quite sympathetic toward it. Many of the young, idealistic students object to the use of petro-chemical products such as plastic and bituminous membranes and polystyrene insulations. To you, I say, "Congratulations, you've got your head screwed on right." I can offer you a couple of suggestions.

First, if you absolutely cannot accept a bituminous or plastic membrane, consider waterproofing instead with natural clay, such as bentonite. When water hits the bentonite, it causes the clay to expand by seven times its original volume, creating hydrostatic pressure so great that water cannot penetrate beyond the first few thousand molecular layers. Maeshowe, the 5,000-year-old neolithic burial chamber in Orkney, stayed dry 4,000 years thanks to clay waterproofing, until the Vikings broke in by punching a hole in the roof.

As for the extruded polystyrene, it will be possible to get the sauna up to temp (and keep it that way) with a roof constructed just of 2-inch planking and covered with an honest 6 inches of earth and, finally, grass. Such a roof holds snow better than any other kind, too, and new light fluffy snow is worth R-1 per inch of thickness. Yet the extruded polystyrene will provide useful extra insulation, making the sauna more comfortable and saving fuel. Extruded polystyrenes are now made without chlorofluorocarbons (CFCs; those nasty ozone-eating molecules that were of so much concern—rightfully—a few years ago) as the expanding agent, making foam boards far less environmentally harmful than they used to be.

I have one last comment on these environmental questions. The one layer that I would absolutely not leave out of the earth roof design is the drainage layer, which takes most of the pressure off of whatever membrane you choose. And that means keeping the 12 by 16-foot sheet of 6-mil black poly, which probably has far fewer petrochemicals in it than, say, a telephone. Just living in the western world means that we contribute to pollution. If a product extends the life of a building, as the black plastic does, or minimizes the energy consumption of the building, as the polystyrene does . . . well, these are valuable considerations in the large scheme of things.

THE SAWDUST CONCRETE FLOOR

I wish I could claim the sawdust concrete idea as my own, but I can't. Back in the 1970s, I had heard—little more than a rumor—that Cornell University was doing research on sawdust concrete. Based on that scant information, I conducted my own experiment at the Log End Sauna. I wanted a floor that would drain washwater away without de-

3-16. The stoveroom at Log End Sauna is formed out for the four triangular sections of sawdust concrete. All four facets slope down to the cast iron drain at the center.

terioration to the floor itself, and I wanted a floor that was easy on bare feet. Concrete is hard, but, worse, it's cold—in the winter, real cold. I attended to both situations with sawdust concrete, in combination with the drain discussed on page 52. The sawdust concrete mix is 2 parts sand, 2 parts soaked sawdust (prepared as for cordwood mortar), and 1 part Portland cement. Mix the ingredients to a fairly stiff consistency, and you're ready to pour.

The drain, you will recall, was installed so that its top surface is one inch below the level of the concrete ring beam. It is located in the center of the stove room. Washwater runs down to this drain. At Log End Sauna, I created four triangular-shaped facets of sawdust concrete, all sloping toward the center, like an inverted hip roof. It sounds difficult, but was really quite easy.

The four triangles were formed with four short lengths of 2 × 4s placed on the plastic sheet as in figure 3-2. Unlike the footing forms, these little forming pieces stay permanently in place, so it wouldn't be a bad idea to use pressure-treated material for the purpose. I actually used ordinary economy studding left over from other projects, and it has not deteriorated since 1979.

The little forming pieces are set so that their top surfaces start at footing level at the corners, and slope down (at a 1:12 slope) to the center. Lay out a slightly longer piece than necessary, mark its underside with a short pencil, and cut it to fit snugly between the corner and the center drain. For strength, lay triangular pieces of wire mesh reinforcing down on the plastic. Then pour the sawdust concrete.

With your rubber gloves, or the tines of a rake, pull the wire mesh up off the plastic and into the middle of the concrete. Then screed with a 2 × 4 and trowel the triangles as smooth as you can. The high saw-dust content will guarantee a nonskid surface.

THE FLOOR OF THE ANTECHAMBER

A Wood Disk Floor

The antechamber at the original Log End Sauna was never fully closed in. We moved to Earthwood before we got around to it, and the new owners seem happy to use the building as it has existed these past 18 years. Our idea was to install a sliding glass door unit on the tall south-ern (front) exposure, and mosquito screens on the large trapezoidal upper wall areas on the east and west sides. The internally mounted plexiglas windows could fold up to the rafters to provide an airy but bug-free summer room. In the winter, with the plexiglas windows fas-tened down, the room would warm up somewhat on a sunny day just from the solar gain coming in through the south-facing glass door. All of this could still be done.

We actually used the open antechamber space as a porch where we would rest on benches between sessions in the stove room. The floor was simply 3-inch disks of elm set in the sand pad with no mortar be-tween them. We hung a Solar Shower from the highest girder, and

3-17. The antechamber at Log End Sauna features a wood disk floor.

showered right in the antechamber, the water just percolating down through the cordwood floor into the sand pad itself. One might expect that elm disks set in sand like this would not last long, but, in fact, they have stayed in good condition and are still in place today. I credit the percolating sand and the overhead protection for this cordwood floor's longevity. Today, I would approach the antechamber a little differently, and would forego the cordwood floor.

Concrete Floor Options

One option, of course, is to install a sawdust concrete floor, as already described, except that there would be no real need for a drain, so the process would be somewhat easier. After a month of curing, both the stoveroom and antechamber floors can be sealed with a couple of coats of masonry sealer or cement floor paint to minimize dusting of the surface. Slate or tile sealer would work, too, as would any of the clear waterseal-type products.

Another option is a true concrete floor, which could be painted with concrete floor paint or covered with indoor-outdoor carpet. If the concrete floor is desired, it could be poured at the same time as the perimeter footings. Just leave out the southern forming ring on figure 3-2 and pour a reinforced 4-inch-thick floor in that area. This will add about 14.5 cubic feet of concrete—just over one-half cubic yard—to the pour. Reinforce with "6 × 6 × 10 × 10" wire mesh. This cryptic designation, known to most building suppliers, means that the gridwork of the mesh is 6 inches in each direction, and the wire gauge is #10 in each direction. You can buy a single 5- by 10-foot sheet of the stuff. It is quite inexpensive and will hold the whole floor together in case it cracks for any reason.

The Instant Slate Floor

We came up with what I think is a very exciting floor option at the Earthwood Guest House, which I call the "Instant Slate Floor." Prior to the cement truck's arrival, Jaki, son Rohan, and I prepared a sufficient quantity of recycled roofing slates—about 80—to cover the entire exposed floor, with one-inch joints between slates. Preparation consisted of applying Acryl-60 bonding agent (Thoro System Products, 7800 N.W. 38th St., Miami, FL 33166) to the underside of the slates, as seen in figure 3-4. This is the side that had been exposed to

100 years or more of weathering on the roof. Flipping the slates over like this reveals a surface in better condition than the weathered side, and eliminates the dangerous splintery top edge of the slate which might rip the skin off the bottom of bare feet.

After the floating slab was poured, screeded, and roughly troweled, I spaced roofing nails along the north and south forming boards, corresponding to the courses of slate that we intended to lay. The nails, then, set with about ¾-inch revealed, marked both edges of each mortar joint between slates. We joined the nails along the lengthwise axis of the building with tightly stretched nylon mason's line, defining the joints very accurately. Then, with a rubber mallet, Rohan and I began to set the slates in place, leaving the same inch between slates on the north-south axis.

We soon found that the concrete was still too wet to work with. The plastic under the pour does a good job of retarding the set. We downed tools and welcomed the break after the hard work of the pour. It was nearly two hours before the concrete was the right consistency to set the slates. Then we installed the 80-odd slates in a little over half an hour, using sheets of plywood or foamboard to reach the work toward the center. The process is simple. Just tap the slates firmly into the concrete with the rubber mallet, until "mud" begins oozing up between slates. Make sure that you can't hear the hollow sound of any air voids under the slates. For visual interest, we even included a number of round slates in the floor, cut from larger damaged slates using a borrowed slate cutter.

3-18. Using a rubber hammer, the author sets old roofing slates into the still-plastic concrete.

3-19. Jaki points the mortar between slates.

Next, Chief Pointer Jaki, Rohan, and I pointed the whole floor with our cordwood masonry pointing knives, being careful to leave no sharp edges of slate exposed. The pointing took about an hour and a half. So, all told, with two extra hours of work on the day of the slab pour, we have a finished floor for the entire Guest House, a floor of great texture, character, and beauty. That's as close to instant as it gets. We have had a similar floor downstairs at Earthwood since 1981. We love it and guests marvel at the expensive appearance. In reality, the floor cost next to nothing and maintenance consists of a quick application of slate floor sealer once every year or two.

If you are really crafty, and make good use of a slate cutting tool, it would be possible to incorporate such a slate floor—even with a center drain—into the stoveroom. It would be much colder to the feet, though, than the sawdust concrete.

FRAMING FOR WINDOWS, DOORS, AND VENTS

A small amount of wall framing defines the location and size of any windows, doors, or vents in the sauna building, and must be installed before work on any of these features or the cordwood masonry itself can commence. The suggested floor plan given in figure 3-1 for the stove room and antechamber, including placement of doors, windows,

3-20. The antechamber at Log End Sauna could easily be closed in to provide a dressing room as well as a wintertime relaxation area.

and vents, can be altered to meet individual circumstances, including the accommodation of doors or windows you might already have or can secure inexpensively. Exterior quality doors should be used, and windows, at least in the stove room, should be insulated glass (double-pane).

The original Log End Sauna used cordwood masonry exclusively for the three exterior walls of the stove room. The antechamber has a rough-cut 2 × 8 divider about midway up the east and west exterior walls. The single 4-inch-thick insulated door was positioned midway between the east and west walls. It was framed by the central girder above and two 8 × 8 barn beam posts on either side. These 6-foot, 6-inch posts are in addition to the six described in the frame material list. They don't have to be that heavy. At the Guest House, we framed the door with four-by-eights.

On either side of the door, we installed identical 1-inch insulated glass window units. These windows do not open. They face south into the antechamber, so heat loss is kept to a minimum. The door also has a window and opens into the antechamber. So, the parts of the stove room walls with the greatest heat loss—door and windows—face the antechamber. This cuts way down on heat loss, particularly if the antechamber is closed in.

At the Guest House, we wanted to make use of two recycled, trape-

3-21. The Guest House would make a great sauna, with a stoveroom to the rear and a relaxation room just inside the front door.

zoidal, fixed thermal pane windows, so we installed horizontal 4 × 8s at the right height to accommodate these windows. We continued the lines of these members right into the front half of the building, which would be the antechamber in a sauna design. Later, the four cordwood panels below these horizontal members each featured a huge 52-inch-diameter log-end at its center.

We built the Guest House door on the south side of the building, choosing a door width that allowed us to make use of two inexpensive double-hung insulated glass units. We framed the door with 4 × 8s, maintaining a certain consistency of architecture. Two 22- by 24-inch fixed thermal pane units, bought for $10 each at a local manufacturer of insulated glass, were installed in rough-cut 2 × 8 frames, which were then "floated" in the cordwood panels above the horizontal dividers.

The point here is to make use of components that you can recycle or purchase cheaply. Plan any needed dividers to accommodate these components, but try to retain a consistency of architectural style. The use of rough-cut, full-sized material, for example, instead of modern "finished" lumber, makes a big difference. If I give you a materials list specifying a certain size of window or door, it will drive the cost of your sauna way up. You can spend several hundred dollars on windows and doors, or, like our Guest House, built in 1995–1996, you can spend about $300.

Here is a tip that could save you hundreds of dollars. For low-cost sauna windows, go to the nearest manufacturer of insulated glass, and ask to see any units that they have left over, usually leaning against the wall in some back room. These are units that were cut the wrong size, or never paid for, or never collected by the customer for some reason. The manufacturer is happy to sell them for a fraction of their original price, just to get rid of them. It is not economical to take them apart, clean the glass, and cut smaller units from the pieces. With cordwood masonry, you can use all sorts of odd-shaped units. As the Log End Sauna design is based on symmetry, though, try to find paired units. Then design your dividers (frames) and door width to accommodate these bargains.

Another window idea, this one from Tom Johnson and Tim Miller's *The Sauna Book*, is to screw and glue together two same-sized recycled wooden-framed window units, making a low-cost "insulated glass" unit.

I've used three different systems for making vents in a sauna wall. Two involve tricks of cordwood masonry discussed in chapter six, but

3-22. This vent features a mosquito screen.

the other is appropriate here. A sauna vent can consist of a frame of rough-cut 2 × 8s that are either "floated" in the cordwood masonry wall like a large log-end or can be installed next to a window, as we did at the Guest House. Sometimes a vent can be used as a space filler between a window and a vertical or horizontal timber. Make it to fit. For a vent cover, just mount a piece of 2-inch (R-10) extruded polystyrene to a wooden cover, put a handle on it, and you're in business. The polystyrene should friction-fit snugly into the vent opening. Make it as fancy as you like. At the Guest House, we refined the process to include a mosquito screen. Instead of a solid 2 × 8 frame, two identical 2 × 4 frames sandwich the screen. In a sauna, you can open an unscreened vent without fear. I have yet to meet the mosquito who likes 180-degree heat.

CORDWOOD MASONRY
AT LOG END SAUNA

Masonry walls can enclose a space by any of three ways: by curving (discussed in the next chapter), by meeting at stackwall, or "built-up," corners (shown in figure 4-19), or by simply filling the spaces within a heavy post-and-beam frame. We used this latter style with the Log End Sauna design. All three methods make use of the basic techniques described in chapter two, but each has its own special considerations.

With the Log End Sauna design, you will sometimes have to fit the cordwood masonry into rather tight quarters, particularly as the work approaches the top of a panel framed by heavy timbers. Normally you have plenty of room to build onto the cordwood masonry from above. This starts to seem like a bit of a luxury as you get closer to a girder or rafter at the top of the wall. On the way there, though, you will have gained some valuable experience fitting the masonry against vertical posts. You may have had to split log-ends to fit a particular space. You will have learned to place the sawdust insulation in awkward, hard-to-reach spots. On the last course of cordwood masonry before you hit the beam, you may have to pour the insulation between mortar joints with a small tin can.

You may also need help from a partner on the other side of the wall for placing the last log-ends in their spaces, because you can't see, from one side of the wall, whether or not the log-end is too close to the beam on the other side. An assistant might be able to help work the log-end down into the outer mortar joint, or suggest a different size or shape of log, or mark it with a pencil for adjustment. It is quicker and more visually satisfying to split one clear-grained log-end down to the proper shape than it is to fill the gap with a hodge-podge of little bits and pieces.

After you have installed the last course of cordwood, the remaining problem is to fill the gap between that course and the top beam with mortar and insulation. Here, we must depart from the "mortar, then insulation" dictum: the insulation obviously must go in first. And loose fill insulation such as sawdust is impossible to place in this final gap, as gravity is working against us.

The answer to the problem is to jam the middle third of the gap with some other type of insulation. I have had good luck with both fiberglass and bits of rigid polystyrene. Use eye and nose protection while cutting fiberglass into strips. And use your gloved hand to stuff the insulation into the middle third of the wall between the last log-ends and the beam. With polystyrene insulation, it is easiest to cut the material to size with a handsaw. Then, again, stuff it in. Whatever material you use, jam it in there fairly tightly. The insulation doubles as a resistance for the mortar to come.

The last bead of mortar is pushed into place off the back of a trowel, either with your gloved fingers or with a pointing knife. If the insulation was snugly jammed, you will be able to push the mortar into this gap with good pressure and it won't break through to the other side.

3-23. Jaki jams the space above the last course of log-ends with fiberglass insulation.

WINDOWS AND DOORS

The key to installing windows is to have the correct rough opening. Always have the windows on site to try them prior to the final fastening of any rough framing pieces, such as heavy timbers. If purchasing manufactured units, don't believe any of the several different dimensions listed in the manufacturer's literature. Consider them all lies. HAVE THE WINDOW ON HAND!

With fixed thermal pane units, create the rough opening so that its dimensions are ½ inch greater in each direction than the outside dimensions of the unit itself. If the unit measures 25½ by 35½ inches, for example, make the rough opening 26 by 36 inches. This allows for ¼ inch of air space all around the unit. The bottom of the unit should rest on a ¼-inch rubber shim made for the purpose. If you can't find these, shims cut from wooden shingles also work well. Don't use metal shims, which will break the glass.

I like to keep the window toward the outside of the thick cordwood wall. This prevents standing water on the window sill and provides a useful shelf on the interior. The least expensive window trim casing is plain 1 × 1 stock, ripped from a pine or cedar board. If working from the inside of the building, install the outer casing first, using small finish nails or, better, screws. Start with the upper and lower pieces with only one screw at the mid-point of the lower piece, so that it can pivot. Then place a couple of the rubber or wooden shims on the base of the rough opening, tight to the casing. You can check that the upper and lower casing pieces are in the same plane by trying the window. If the window doesn't touch both pieces without a gap or a wobble, make the necessary adjustment to the lower 1 × 1 casing piece. Then install the side casing pieces, the window itself, and the four inner casing pieces. Caulk with clear siliconized caulking if there are gaps.

If using an existing exterior-quality door, it is important to frame the rough opening to fit. Again, a quarter inch (¼") all around the door is a good tolerance, perhaps a half inch (½") at the bottom for safety's sake. If the door is prehung, great. Just shim the prehung frame plumb within your rough opening and then trim it out, perhaps with the same 1 × 1 stock recommended for the windows. Install new weatherstripping, if needed. I have had good luck with the sticky-backed weatherstripping, although it needs to be renewed every few years.

Our sauna doors are homemade. They are heavily insulated and

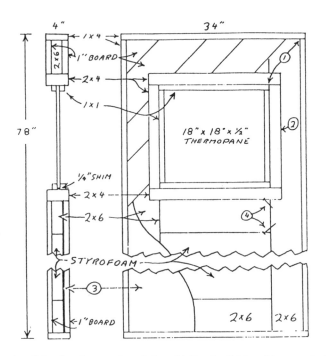

3-24. A well-insulated sauna door design. (1) Caulk all joints (2) 2 × 4 window framing (3) 6-mil plastic under outside sheathing (4) 2 × 6 framework held with toenails until 1-inch sheathing is fixed to both sides of door.

make use of rough-cut material to match the rustic style of the sauna. We include a window (insulated glass, of course) whenever possible. A window in a sauna door lets you monitor the arrival of fellow bathers, for example, and may provide a view different from any others in the sauna, depending on the plan. The illustration shows a heavy 4-inch-thick door of a type we have built time and again, for houses as well as saunas. We hang such doors with three heavy (10-inch) T-hinges. On the strike side of the door, we allow a half-inch clearance instead of a quarter inch, to accommodate its exceptional thickness. Use wooden shingles under the heavy door to hold it fairly tight against the top and the hinged side of the frame. Then lag screw the heavy T-hinges to both the frame and the door. When the shingles are removed, the "play" in the hinges will allow the door to pull away slightly from the frame and the door will swing properly. With these homemade doors, I install a door stop made of 1 × 1 for the door to close against from the outside. Only the bottom of the door does not close against a door stop.

Sauna doors must always open out for safety and shouldn't have locks. Doors supplied with manufactured sauna cabinets usually come supplied with a special mechanism for holding the door closed. Some of the suppliers listed in Appendix One sell prehung insulated sauna doors, both with and without windows. Some actually sell the mechanism which holds the door closed, but the old-fashioned screen door catch, available at hardware stores, will do the same job.

SAUNA PLATFORMS

The sauna platform (often called a bench in the U.S.) is where the bather sits. It is, therefore, one of the stoveroom's most important structural features. A large sauna may have several platforms installed at different heights to provide bathers with a choice of temperature: the nearer the ceiling, the hotter the air.

The Log End Sauna design includes a bench on either side of the centrally-located woodstove, both at the same height. For the most part, Jaki and I make use of the building as a two-passenger sauna, so we each have our own private platform. The sauna easily accommodates four, however, and we have even managed five or six at times, but bathers must sit in these circumstances, no lounging around. The platforms could be set at different heights, of course, to give a temperature option. Another possible layout would be to put the stove on one side of the room and two platforms of different heights on the opposite side. We find that having the platforms facing each other contributes to sociability.

Whatever plan you choose, construction of the platforms is pretty much the same. The first and most important consideration is the selection of wood for the benches themselves. The wood chosen should have a low conductivity of heat. In general, this means avoiding densely grained woods such as maple, oak, and most other hardwoods. The best species for the purpose, if available, is poplar, also known as quaking aspen. Considered a "junk wood" by many, it is available throughout the northern states (perhaps on your own woodlot) and logs can usually be purchased quite inexpensively.

Cottonwood, with similar characteristics to poplar, is another good choice. I have used white cedar with success, and (in Scotland) Czechoslovakian red pine, not readily available in North America. If the aspen is not available, I would choose clear-grained spruce, or red, white, or jack pine. Knots will be hard, hot, and pitchy. If the planks you install do happen to bleed, don't despair. After a few saunas—and a little scraping between saunas—the pitch will eventually disappear.

In Finland, aspen and spruce are the popular choices for platforms. American manufacturers of prefab saunas use western red cedar, Idaho white pine, Alaska yellow cedar, Finnish pine, western hemlock, and redwood for both platforms and cabinet walls. The use of redwood raises certain environmental questions, in my view, and redwood also tends to stain from the perspiration, which spoils its attractive appearance. Pines, spruce, and cedar all have pleasant aromas. Incense or aromatic cedar is too strong. Aspen is virtually odorless. Avoid splintery woods, particularly Eastern hemlock. And definitely don't use pressure-treated decking.

As for dimensions, I like a sturdy platform surface made of 2 × 6 stock, planed on all four sides. The planing process will typically reduce the dimensions to 1¾ × 5¾. Unplaned or "rough cut" lumber would be intolerably uncomfortable to sit on and very absorbant of perspiration. You might even consider the use of ordinary "finished" 2 × 6 framing material, as long as it is fairly knot-free. The advantage of nominal 2 × 6 material, as opposed to 1-inch, is that greater planking spans can be employed. With the Log End Sauna design, the benches can span from wall to wall—6 feet—without the need for an intermediate support. Eliminating supports makes for easy construction as well as easy cleaning of the stove room.

The platform can be supported by the cordwood wall itself. Simply screw two pieces of the same 2 × 6 bench deck material right to the cordwood wall, at lengths equal to the desired width of the platform (typically 24 inches), and at the desired height off the floor. Our present sauna has platforms at 36 and 42 inches off the floor. If both platforms are on the same side of the room, 24- and 42-inch heights are recommended. The lower bench serves as a step to the upper platform. In family saunas where three platforms are used on the same side, the bench heights are 16, 32, and 48 inches.

Here are some tips on screwing a plank to the cordwood wall:

1. Using a level, hold the nailer piece—known as a *ledger*—at its intended height and, with a pencil, mark the location of the top of the ledger on the log-ends themselves. Mark the locations of five or six screws for a 24-inch-long ledger, keeping screw locations well away from the edges of both the ledger and log-ends. Try to fasten to the larger log-ends. As a cord-

3-25 A wooden ledger, screwed to several log-ends, provides support for the platform planks.

wood wall can be 40 percent mortar, care should be taken in marking these screw locations. You can't screw into mortar.

2. For adequate shear strength, use ⁵⁄₁₆-inch hex-headed lag screws, at least four inches long. With an assistant holding the nailer firmly in place, pre-drill holes through the ledger and into the log-ends. Use a bit slightly smaller than the size of the lag screws — ¼-inch bit for a ⁵⁄₁₆-inch screw.

3. If shoddy cordwood work has left a log-end too long, making it difficult to hold the ledger relatively flat to the wall, trim the offending piece with a chainsaw. Likewise, overly recessed log-ends can be built out with a spacer made from a piece of board or plywood of appropriate thickness. Fasten any such spacer securely to the log-end. The best advice here is to concentrate (during cordwood construction) on keeping log-ends in the same plane on the interior of the building. Any irregularity in log-end length should be left to the exterior, where it won't do any harm. This also prevents an awkward log-end from sticking a bather in the back.

With the ledgers firmly in place, installing the platform deck is as easy as measuring, cutting, and screwing the planks into place. Ordinary wood screws can be used here, countersunk so that no one ever sits on a hot screw. Leave a quarter inch between planks for perspiration to run through. Thus, four 5¾-inch-wide planks will give you a 24-inch-wide platform.

Spans greater than 6 feet will require an internal platform support.

This can be made of another ledger, installed flat-wise this time, with one end supported by the cordwood wall (use a miniledger here) and the other end by an appropriate post, such as another piece of 2 × 6 or, perhaps, a 4-inch-diameter vertical log.

Some people like back rests to lean on. Although we have not found back rests to be strictly necessary, a really rough-textured cordwood wall might be more comfortable to lean against if rests made from horizontal wooden pieces are installed. These small boards or slats can be an inch or less thick and any convenient width: 4 inches, 6 inches, whatever. Again, use wood of low conductivity, the same as for the platform itself. And countersink those screws.

To conclude this chapter, let's examine how a couple from cold Saskatchewan took a somewhat different approach to a cordwood sauna within a framework of recycled timbers.

CLIFF AND JACKIE SHOCKEY'S DOUBLE-WALL CORDWOOD SAUNA

For nearly twenty years Cliff Shockey has been in the forefront of Canada's cordwood masonry movement. In 1993, Cliff's unique "double-wall" technique won the energy-efficient house design competition sponsored by *Harrowsmith Magazine*, "Canada's Magazine of Country Living." In brief, Cliff's method is to build two separate and relatively narrow cordwood shells, one within the perimeter of the other, with fiberglass insulation between the two walls. With his recommended cold-climate 24-inch-thick house walls (8-inch cordwood, 8-inch fiberglass, 8-inch cordwood), Cliff has been able to achieve insulation values of R-40. And there is plenty of thermal mass on both sides of the insulation, so the home is cool in summer, warm in winter. His system is just right for Saskatchewan's climate, with its 12,000+ heating degree day units.

In 1993, Cliff and his wife Jackie built a cordwood sauna near their beautiful home in the heart of the great Canadian Plains. Not surprisingly, as fuel wood is not overly plentiful, they stuck with their energy-efficient technique. Further, they employed a simple foundation system requiring no concrete whatsoever. Cliff and Jackie managed to build their eight-by-eight-foot stoveroom (internal dimensions) with large covered porch enclosure for a total of CN$500, less than US$400 at the time of construction. "The steel for the roof was approximately $200," says Cliff. "The treated 2 × 10 foundation and the two sheets of

⅝-inch plywood for the floor cost about $300. The rest of the lumber for the roof and the post-and-beam frame was recycled from old barns I've taken down."

The Shockey Sauna foundation system is fairly self-explanatory in Cliff's own drawings (figures 3-26, 3-27, and 3-28). Sixteen pressure-treated 2 × 10 planks and sixteen posts make up the foundation. Cliff's top view of the foundation (before gravel) shows the location of the members. Six of the pressure-treated sidewall planks are 11 feet (cut from 12-footers, no doubt) and two are 8-footers. Cliff used recycled plastic posts driven into the ground for pilings, but locust or 4 × 4 pressure-treated posts would do. I had never heard of plastic posts in New York, but Cliff assures me that they are a common item in the Great Plains, and, like wood, can receive nails. He advises that the posts be set to local frost level. Once the tracks are formed by the 2 × 10s, they're filled with tamped bank-run gravel or crushed stone. Finally, a double-wide layer of top plates is installed as per the foundation and wall cross-sectional diagram. This double-wide planking system requires four 8-footers and four 11-footers. The completed post-and-beam frame and roof can be seen in the photo (figure 3-29).

The floor is simply recycled 2 × 6s hung on the 2 × 10s with joist hangers, available at any lumber yard. The 6 × 6 posts are installed above the pressure-treated plates as shown in the diagram below. These posts frame the cordwood masonry panels.

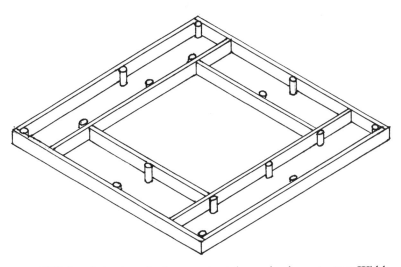

3-26. Cliff's foundation is made of pressure-treated 2 × 12 lumber, as per text. Width of wall is exaggerated in this diagram.

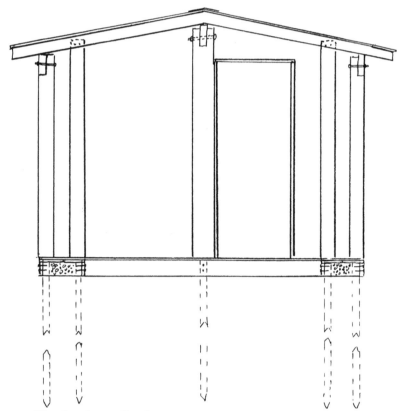

3-27. *Elevation of sauna framing, showing 6 × 6 posts for both the inner and the outer cordwood walls. The door frame is made of rough-cut material. A frame of 2 × 8s standing next to another frame of 2 × 10s, for example, will make up the full 18-inch wall thickness.*

3-28. *Cross section of foundation, wall, and floor. (1) 2 × 10 pressure-treated foundation pieces (2) 4 × 4 pressure-treated or plastic posts set to frost depth (3) ⅝-inch rough plywood (4) ⅝-inch smooth plywood for floor (5) 2 × 6 floor joist (6) Metal joist hanger (7) Tamped gravel (8) 6-inch log-ends (9) mortar (10) 6-mil plastic vapor barrier (11) 6-inch fiberglass batt insulation (12) 5/16-inch particle board or recycled paneling.*

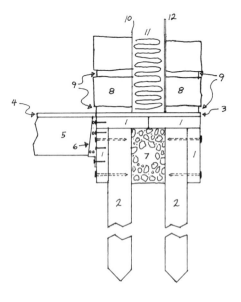

The cordwood work follows these steps:

1. The outer 6-inch cordwood wall is built, using a solid mortar joint through the wall.

2. Inexpensive or recycled hardboard, chipboard, or recycled paneling is installed next to the inner surface of the outer wall.

3. Six-inch fiberglass batts are placed up against the cheap flatboard, with nails protruding from the flatboard to keep the batts in place, if necessary.

4. A vapor barrier is installed on the warm side of the insulation, stapled to the floor, roof rafters, posts, windows, doors, etc. This barrier protects the fiberglass from the sauna steam.

5. The inner 6-inch cordwood wall, again with a solid mortar joint, is installed. The completed 18-inch-thick wall has an R-value of 25 or better.

It is not as time-consuming as you might think. The same number of pointing surfaces are involved, one interior, one exterior. A little more mud needs to be mixed, but there is no sawdust insulation to pour. About the same amount of cordwood is used, although there are twice as many sawcuts to make. Cliff did a double-wall construction demonstration at the 1994 Continental Cordwood Conference at Earthwood Building School, and I was impressed by how fast he could work. See Cliff at work in figure 2-10.

Two 20-foot-long 4 × 6 girders run the length of the sauna, including the added porch overhang. Rough-cut 2 × 6s on 24-inch centers make up the rafter system, with just enough pitch, about three in twelve (3:12), to support the metal roof. An inner ceiling of boards in the stoveroom is topped with a vapor barrier and fiberglass insulation.

Cliff and Jackie like their sauna at around 145 degrees Fahrenheit, easy to maintain with their iron woodstove. "Someday I hope to have a smaller stove," says Cliff. I'm trying to sell him on the virtues of surrounding the iron firebox with bricks or stones to change the sometimes harsh radiant heat to a "softer" conducted and convected heat. "There is one roof vent," says Cliff, "plus a vent in the door. But if it gets too hot, we just open the door. The only window is in the door, but we use electric light as needed and prefer subdued light in the sauna."

For design features, Cliff and Jackie incorporated a sunburst pattern next to the door, rows of bottle ends on the stoveroom sidewalls, and a unique wagon wheel cordwood design on one of the exterior side-

3-29. Cliff and Jackie's sauna. Relaxation takes place in the covered porch area.

3-30. A sunburst design graces the panel next to the door. These four photos are by Cliff Shockey.

walls. As the Shockeys operate a wonderful bed and breakfast in Costa Rica from December to April—which *my* Jaki and I have visited with pleasure—the sauna doesn't get a lot of wintertime use. Therefore, their covered outdoor "porch" is a particularly appropriate feature for their predominantly summertime use. They don't wash in the sauna over their plywood floor, preferring to scamper over to the house for a cooling shower. But there is no reason why a sawdust concrete floor

3-31. *Cliff's recycled wood-burning stove heats the sauna easily.*

3-32. *Jackie Shockey (right) and a friend sweat it out at 145 degrees Fahrenheit.*

and central drain couldn't be substituted for the joists and plywood floor, if washing right in the sauna is desired.

All in all, the Shockey's sauna, which is certainly capable of maintaining its heat during the cold Saskatchewan winter, is a great example of building an effective, pleasant, and low-cost sauna without concrete and with a variety of recycled materials.

· 4 ·

The Earthwood (Round) Sauna

ROUND SAUNAS are unusual. To be perfectly honest, in all my travels and research for this book, I have only come across one that I wasn't involved in myself: a sauna in Connecticut built from a wooden silo. My next-door neighbor's manufactured barrel-shaped sauna doesn't count; although cylindrical, the cylinder rests on its side, and the bathers enter through one of the ends. The plan of the barrel sauna is actually rectilinear.

Why the dearth of round saunas? My theory is that by any construction method other than cordwood masonry, they are just too darned difficult to build. In Finland, the old traditional saunas were built of horizontal logs, not conducive to building a round shape. Maybe this book will get translated into Finnish and Swedish and revolutionize the backyard sauna in Scandinavia.

A round sauna does pose a few problems. Platforms are made from long planks, for example; how can they fit into a round building? I will address any disadvantages peculiar to the round style in this chapter, but I want to begin by accentuating the positives.

ADVANTAGES OF A ROUND SAUNA

Some of the advantages of building round are similar to those cited in chapter two for cordwood masonry itself, but they stem from different reasons. Particularly in combination with cordwood masonry, round is highly distinctive. This is why both our home, Earthwood, and summer camp, Mushwood, are round cordwood buildings.

The advantages of round cordwood buildings are several:

ECONOMY OF CONSTRUCTION. A round building is the most economical to build, particularly when masonry units are used for wall construction. This is simply a reality of geometry and is connected with such phenomena as spherical soap bubbles and even the hexagonal-shaped compartments in a beehive. Almost every one of the building species, except humans, builds round. A bird, for example, has no interest in square corners. She's on deadline. She must build the most comfortable nest as quickly as possible. (Actually, so called "primitive" people built—and build—round houses. It was the advent of city streets and the use of long straight trees as building materials that brought *homo sapiens* around to the present fixation with square corners.) A true square is the most economically efficient of the rectilinear shapes for enclosing space, but cylindrical walls of the same perimeter will actually enclose 27.3 percent more space. As it then costs a little more to roof the greater area, some of this economy is lost; but the building still has more space.

ENERGY-EFFICIENCY. While the cylinder encloses the most space per linear unit of wall perimeter, the same mathematical accident dictates that it requires the least wall or "skin" area to enclose a given volume. Less skin area means less heat loss, so the building is easier to heat. This is true for big buildings, medium buildings, and small (sauna) buildings. Now, I can hear the dome freaks out there screaming, "Domes are the most efficient!" Fair enough. I like domes. The top story of Mushwood is a dome. But if you want to get technical, the sphere from which the dome is taken is truly the most efficient. But we can't live in a bubble; we'll bump our heads. For a species that wanders around vertically, the cylinder makes the best use of space. Besides, domes are harder to build and harder to waterproof.

ATMOSPHERE. Here hard mathematical facts must give way to more esoteric, subjective, and even spiritual arguments. A round sauna provides a womb- or denlike quality that other saunas don't quite match. I didn't know this until we used the Earthwood Sauna for the first time. The building feels right. Perhaps it stirs some prenatal memory in the wispy backwaters of our consciousness. I get the same kind of feeling sitting around the Stone Circle at night, a bonfire crackling in the center. (I warned you this might get metaphysical.) In the Southwest, Pueblo Indian tribes built round kivas of stone or adobe, sometimes wholly or partially underground.

These buildings were used for a variety of spiritual and ceremonial purposes, not the least of which was the male ritual of the sweat lodge. They didn't have to build their kivas round; most of their other dwellings had square corners. I don't think that it's any coincidence that the kivas, stone circles, and megalithic burial chambers, all structures with a connection to the spirit world, were round.

These excellent reasons for building round notwithstanding, our main reason for choosing a round sauna was architectural. We wanted a structure that would be in visual harmony with the round Earthwood house. The Log End Sauna would stick out like the proverbial digit if built right next to a large round house. The other outbuildings in immediate proximity are also round. The net architectural effect is not unlike that of a Zulu village. The Earthwood Guest House, with its rectilinear post-and-beam lines, stands alone in the woods, some distance from the main group of buildings.

This raises the question: Will a round sauna be out of place next to a rectilinear, contemporary home? I don't think so; at least, not as much as the other way around. It can be part of its own little garden architecture, like, say, an octagonal gazebo.

4-1. The round sauna harmonizes with the architecture of the Earthwood home itself.

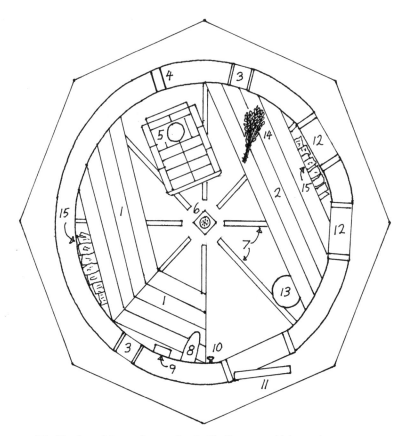

4-2. The Earthwood Sauna has a 9-foot inside diameter, which translates to a 10-foot 4-inch outside diameter with 8-inch log-ends. The octagon roof planking over-hang is 16 inches at the points. Key to drawing:

1. *High platform, 42 inches off floor*
2. *Low platform, 36 inches off floor*
3. *Ceramic thimble (8-inch inside diameter) air vent. A cylindrical log-end closes the vent. Vents are 5 feet and 6 feet off the floor, respectively.*
4. *Four-inch diameter combustion air inlet, near floor*
5. *Stove surrounded by bricks (or stones)*
6. *Floor drain*
7. *Forming boards*
8. *Shelf*
9. *Water resistant (bathroom) light*
10. *Rail spike for thermometer or towel*
11. *2-foot (24-inch) wide door*
12. *16-inch square window*
13. *Wash bucket*
14. *Vihta (whisk)*
15. *Firewood stored under benches*

Drawbacks of the Round Design

There are potential drawbacks to building the round sauna. Let's get them right out on the table.

At Log End Sauna, described in the previous chapter, the post-and-beam frame carries all the load; the cordwood masonry is simply in-filling, not unlike the wattle and daub infilling of Olde English half-timber frame houses. With the round style, however, the cordwood masonry itself supports the roof load. This is not a structural prob-lem—the cordwood masonry is plenty strong enough—but we lose the advantage of being able to get the roof on before the cordwood work is started. With the Log End Sauna design, it might be possible to work during inclement weather. Building in bad weather is more difficult though not impossible with a round building. When we were building a round sauna as a workshop project, for instance, we stretched a large plastic tarp over the entire site so that we could work in any weather.

Another important consideration before deciding on the round de-sign is that the shape of the building is not conducive for subdivision into a stove room and a separate changing or relaxation room. This drawback didn't concern us at Earthwood, because the sauna is just ten feet away from the solar room, which serves as an excellent changing and relaxation area. Your situation, however, might be different. A round sauna standing alone 100 feet from the house might not be as convenient as the Log End Sauna design with its antechamber. An oval design, however, which concludes this chapter, accommodates both a stove room and changing room. Its construction would follow the same general principles described in this chapter.

The Round Foundation

We decided to pour the sauna's relatively small (11 feet in diameter) floating slab "monolithically," which is Stone Age jargon for "in one piece." A pad of sand was built up and compacted in runs, as described in the previous chapter, until the pad was about 8 inches above sur-rounding grade. Then I sculpted a 4-inch-deep by 10-inch-wide track around the perimeter, using a square-tipped shovel. To get the correct location of this track, simply describe two circles in the sand with a sharp stick. The outer circle will have a radius of 5 feet, 6 inches (half of the 11-foot diameter) and the inner circle will have a radius 9 inches less, or 4 feet, 9 inches. The center point can be a small nail protruding slightly from a wooden stake at the center of the building. You can hook your tape measure on the nail. Place the excavated sand just outside the perimeter of the slab location.

Round buildings are no more difficult to build than square ones; in fact, in my experience, they're easier. The important measurements are taken off the center. Retain the center point, and you'll be all right. Lose the center point, and you're going to have a problem.

An innovation which was quite successful at the Earthwood sauna was to form the edge of the pour with an inch of extruded polystyrene, Dow Styrofoam Blueboard, in our case. An 8-inch-wide by 8-foot-long strip of the Blueboard bends around this curvature quite easily. We used plenty of wooden stakes around the perimeter to guard against concrete blow-out. After the Styrofoam forms were set in their place and leveled, we raked the loose sand (which had come from the footing track) up against the Styrofoam form for extra support. Then we chamferred the inner edge of the footing track, as shown in the cross-sectional diagram on page 113. This minimizes the chance of a shear crack forming as shown in the inset. We actually lined the entire slab pour with 1 inch of Styrofoam in an effort to create a warmer floor in the sauna. Had I not used the Styrofoam, I would have at least placed a layer of 6-mil black polyethylene for the purpose of retarding the set. Styrofoam, which is close-celled, also slows transfer of the concrete's moisture to the sand pad.

4-3. The floating slab of the Earthwood Sauna is formed with 1 inch of Dow Styrofoam Blueboard, which is left in place to provide perimeter insulation.

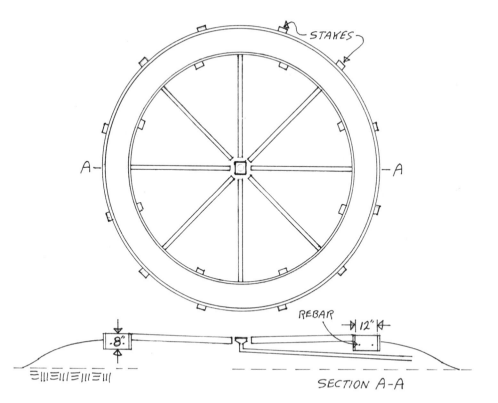

STAKES

A— —A

REBAR

SECTION A-A

4-4. Earthwood Sauna Foundation Notes

(1) *Scrape topsoil to the edge of site, for use later on the roof.*
(2) *Build up the sand pad in runs of 4 inches at a time, to a depth of about 16 inches after compaction.*
(3) *Form with quarter-inch plywood ripped into 8-inch strips, or use an inch of extruded polystyrene. Frequent stakes are necessary in either case to maintain a round perimeter and to prevent concrete "blow out" during the pour.*
(4) *Install two pieces of half-inch (#4) rebar in the lower half of the pour, as shown. Keep rebar at least 2 inches from the edge of the pour.*
(5) *After the footings have cured 24 hours, pie-shaped sections of sawdust concrete can be formed with 2 × 4s.. Maintain a 2-inch slope down to the drain in the center, which can be installed prior to pouring the footings. The sauna washwater is drained to some point above grade if contours allow or to a stone-filled soakaway pit.*

This drawing reminds me of a Yogi Berra story. When a waitress asked Yogi if he'd like his pizza cut into four pieces or eight, Yogi is said to have replied, "Better make it four, I don't think I can eat eight."

An alternative to extruded polystyrene as forming material is ¼-inch plywood. Any wooden form heavier than that is difficult to bend around the tight curvature.

We installed a single ring of ½-inch reinforcing bar in the lower half of the thickened edge of the slab, and fitted some 6 × 6 × 10 × 10 wire mesh from one side of the monolithic slab to the other. The purpose of the mesh is to hold the concrete together in case it cracks.

Our round foundation for the Earthwood sauna had a great idea incorporated into its design, a great idea that failed because I didn't pay attention to detail on the day of the pour. With proper attention, however, the idea should work fine.

The intent was to create a floor with the shape of a very shallow martini glass. A drain at the center of the floor would correspond to the stem of the glass. The floor would slope from every point on the building's perimeter to the drain at the center. The plan was to set the drain about an inch below the surface of the slab at its perimeter. As the building was about 11 feet in diameter, all parts of the floor would have a pitch of about one inch for every 5 feet, 6 inches, down toward the center. I figured that with fairly stiff concrete, we could screed from the outside edge of the foundation down to the center drain to create the martini glass shape.

In the event, we were thwarted by two circumstances. First, I forgot to wire the drain to the drainpipe below. Second, the concrete

4-5. We pour the slab at Earthwood Sauna.

came out of the truck far too soupy—a 6-inch slump when we needed a 3-inch—and wouldn't hold even the very gradual one-inch pitch we wanted. This concrete wanted to lay flat. The combination of these circumstances caused the cast iron drain to actually float in the concrete, eliminating any chance of creating a pitch. The floor came out nice and flat, practically useless for draining water. Had the drain been wired down, and perhaps staked with a small piece of ½-inch rebar, and had the concrete been stiff, then maybe the plan would have worked. We corrected the situation after the sauna was built by pouring a new floor of stiff sawdust concrete over the slab. (This is described later.)

We poured the round sauna slab on the same day that we poured the footings for the Earthwood house, so we just ordered an extra 1.2 cubic yards, avoiding the small load charge. Aside from the martini glass fiasco, everything went smoothly. The Styrofoam didn't blow out, and is still in place to this day, helping to arrest heat loss at that important edge-of-slab location.

An alternative to pouring the footings and floor monolithically is to pour the footings with genuine concrete one day and to form out and pour sloping sections of sawdust concrete later, as described in the previous chapter and again with the oval design appearing at the end of this chapter.

CORDWOOD IN THE ROUND

When cordwood masonry will be load-bearing, one of the first jobs is to install the door frame. That way you can concentrate on the masonry without worrying about building right through the door location.

The sauna door can be framed with 4 × 8s for an 8-inch-thick wall; use 4 × 10s if you want 9- or 10-inch walls. On the sides of the frame that will face the cordwood masonry, install a key piece of 1 × 2 or 1 × 3 scrap wood vertically in the middle third of the frame, on the edge of the frame hidden by the masonry. This piece helps tie the door frame to the cordwood wall. The mortar will be laid tight to the door frame, but the unit will be "keyed in" to the masonry with that piece of scrap material. You can employ a similar technique on the lateral sides of window frames. This key piece also stops drafts should the heavy timber door frame shrink away from the cordwood masonry a little.

Our door frame's inner opening is 2 feet by 6 feet, 6 inches. It is very important to make sure that you make the frame wide enough that the stove you have in mind will fit through it. Plumb the frame in both directions (right and left, in and out) with the plumb bubble of a 4-foot level. Drive a couple of stout wooden stakes firmly in the ground about 4 feet from the foundation, and install temporary diagonal braces from the stakes back to the top of the door frames.

Now you are ready for cordwood.

Work from the inside. Mark the inner circumference of the wall on the slab with a brightly colored wax crayon. As the inner diameter is 9 feet, 6 inches, use a 4 foot, 9 inch radius to scribe the circle. Now is a good time to mark on the slab the location of any windows, vents, or special design features that you have in mind. Include a height dimension to the underside of the feature—52" TO VENT, for example—in bright red numbers. These crayon marks will remind you to include these special features in the wall. Without them, it is all too easy to build right through the spot where a window, vent, shelf, or special log-end is supposed to go.

Use the inner circumference as a guide for laying the first course of log-ends. Incorporate a 4- to 6-inch air inlet pipe on the first or second course close to the stove location. Schedule 40 (¼-inch wall) PVC or ABS plastic pipe works well, but almost any 4- to 6-inch-diameter pipe will do. (Other means of providing combustion air to the stove are discussed in chapter five.)

Succeeding courses are kept vertical by the frequent use of a 4-foot level. I don't check every single log-end in the whole building for plumb. My personal rule is to check every fifth piece or so, the 20 percent of the log-ends that are the largest. Use these big ones, carefully plumbed, as guides for all the others. Keep the inner ends of the log-ends in the same plane, letting any variation in length occur on the exterior. This simplifies keeping the wall plumb during construction, facilitates the installation of platform nailers later, and prevents a bather from getting stabbed in the back by an errant log-end.

Really, that is all there is to it until you get near plate height. Follow the same cordwood building techniques described in chapter two. Have any window or vent frames premade and just "float" them in the masonry like oversized log-ends. Don't forget the scrap-wood key pieces on the right and left sides of any window frames.

PLATES

A series of 2 × 8 wooden plates at the top of the cordwood wall provide the transition from cordwood masonry to the radial rafter system used with round cordwood buildings. The plates can also be used to establish a pitch from one side of the roof to the other, important for drainage with an earth roof. Here is how we built and installed the sixteen plates at the Earthwood Sauna:

To figure the plate size, I divided the 29.84-foot inner circumference (9.5-foot diameter x 3.14 = 29.84 feet) by 16 (29.84 ÷ 16), which gave me this rather obtuse number: 1.865 feet. This is slightly (about ⅜ inch) more than 1 foot, 10 inches, so I rounded it down. Removing the ⅜ inch gives me a little "play" in the actual setting of the plates.

I cut 16 plates from rough-cut 2 × 8 stock, each exactly 22 inches long. Next, to provide a little "grab" to the underside of the plates, I set five roofing nails about 1½ inches back from each edge of the plate. I drove them within a half-inch of home. The fully revealed nail heads do a great job of tying the plate to the mortar.

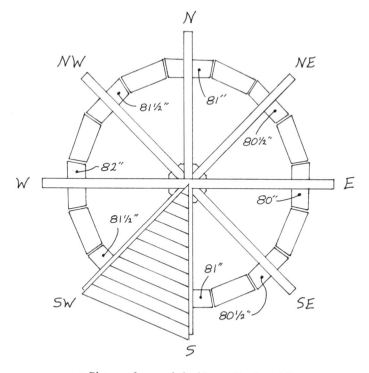

4-6. Plates, rafters, and planking at Earthwood Sauna.

4-7. Smaller (12-inch wide) plates worked well at our office building, which is also earth-roofed.

To establish a slight pitch to the roof, I set the lowest plate, the one on the east "side" of the building, at exactly 80 inches of height to the top of the plate. This measurement corresponds to the underside of the rafter. A little cordwood planning is necessary to achieve such accuracy, but, by now, we have developed some pretty good masonry skills, so never fear. Next, I set the highest plate, the one on the west side, directly opposite the first one, at 82 inches to the top of the plate. Then the north and south plates go in at equal heights of 81 inches. Measure carefully to center these with respect to the east and west plates. The northeast and southeast plates are set at 80½ inches and the southwest and northwest plates at 81½ inches.

The eight plates now in place will carry the eight rafters in the wagon-wheel roof support system. In my round sauna, I actually installed the remaining nonload-bearing plates as well, because it made the "snowblocking" easier to install later on. Snowblocking is installed (and explained) right after we do the rafters.

I am sure that the eight nonload-bearing plates could be eliminated in favor of continuous cordwood masonry right up to the underside of the planking, as we did at the 20-foot-diameter office building at Earthwood (see figure 4-7). I am equally sure that the bearing plates need be no longer than 12 inches, which means that all eight could be cut from a single 8-foot plank. It's up to the builder, really. I went with the elaborate plate system described because I wanted to make use of certain special snowblocking logs, as will be seen.

THE WAGON WHEEL ROOF

Normally, with a radial rafter system (which I feel is the easiest and best for use with a round cordwood building) a heavy post in the center receives the inner end of each rafter. We can't have a post in the middle of this small sauna. So how do we provide necessary structural support at the center?

We can't, unfortunately, simply have one rafter span the building and support the others, because a single 4 × 8 rafter cannot carry its own load as well as the loads of the other six rafters that would meet it. One solution (suggested by a student) is to beef up the primary rafter. You could do this by laying two 4 × 8 rafters side by side, or using a single 8 × 8 girder. Unfortunately, this solution throws the symmetry of the building off kilter, and I don't care for the appearance.

I prefer a wagon-wheel rafter design that uses steel plates to create a strong sandwiched hub at the center. To build this wagon-wheel design, position a 13-foot-long primary rafter (a 4 × 8, like the others) loosely on the centers of the east and west plates. Position the six secondary rafters, each only half as long, with one end on their plates and their "center" ends supported by a temporary post. Cut their innermost ends with a slight bias off of the vertical so that the top (compression) side of the rafters is longer and will bear more strongly against the primary rafter than the bottom (tension) side.

Have a machine shop fabricate two octagonal plates, each 16 inches across, out of ¼-inch plate steel, as in the illustration below. When you

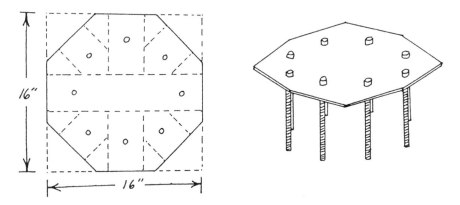

4-8. (left) Pattern for cutting an octagon from a 16-inch piece of 1/4-inch plate steel. Two are required. (right) The nuts on top of the 1/2-inch threaded rods are welded to the top plate. A second plate joins with this octagonal "table," sandwiching the rafters between the plates.

4-9. The wagon wheel roof support system. Note "snowblocks."

4-10. The lower plate is fastened to the upper plate with 1/2-inch nuts.

have them, draw the meeting of the six secondary rafters to the primary rafter to scale on the metal plates and drill eight ½-inch holes
through one of the plates, as shown in figure 4-8. Then mark and drill
corresponding holes through the rafters, taking care to go through the
8 inches of wood as straight as possible.

Next, have eight pieces of ½ × 10-inch threaded rod welded into the holes of the plate, creating a little eight-legged metal table (see figure 4-8). Slide the table legs into the holes in the rafters from above; the tight fit should allow removal of the temporary post.

Now mark the second plate at the points where the threaded rods come through the bottom sides of the rafters; carefully drill the holes, and attach the bottom plate with ½-inch nuts. (Note: Welding the other end of the rods to the top plate, instead of fastening with nuts, allows these bottom nuts to be tightened later as the rafters shrink in the dry sauna heat.) The spokes of the wagon wheel now form a monolithic unit, joined by the strong double-plate hub system. All of the rafters are now load-bearing. The center of the wheel cannot sag without stretching the bottom plate and compressing the top sides of the rafters—neither of which can occur.

Snowblocking

The outer ends of the heavy wagon wheel support structure simply rest on the plates located at the eight primary compass points. They can be toe-screwed to the plate from above (I prefer screwing to the impact load of driving toenails into the wooden plates) but, frankly, the wagon wheel is so heavy that it doesn't really require any fastening at all. Heavy four-inch-wide rough-cut rafters bearing on rough-cut plates don't tend to move, and certainly can't after the snowblocking, planking, and heavy earth roof are installed.

"Snowblocking" is the term used to describe the space between rafters on old timber-frame buildings. Filling this space blocks snow from blowing in. The snowblock infilling at the sauna, seen in figure 4-11, was created quickly by using short pieces of logs, each milled on two sides to a uniform 6-inch thickness. The pieces were leftovers from a friend's log cabin. The logs were laid perpendicular to the usual direction of log-ends in cordwood masonry. The unmilled edges of the logs are exposed to view, rather than the end-grain seen with ordinary log-ends. Securing these in place with a uniform one-inch mortar joint above and below the horizontal log pieces proved to be a very quick method of filling in the pesky snowblock detail on the eight-inch-wide wall.

The snowblock infilling is most easily accomplished before the planking goes on, while access from above is available. Simply lay out a 1-inch bed of mud on the sixteen-sided plate system, set the short pieces of horizontal logs (leaving a mortar joint between each), and finish the top with another inch of mud. The top layer of mud can be screeded flat between rafters with a straight 5-foot-long two-by plank. After the mud stiffens a little, it can be pointed against the same short plank, which is then removed. Later, the roof planking will perfectly meet this flat top edge of the mortar, with nary a gap. You can see in figure 4-11 that we didn't bother with the sawdust-insulated gap on this topmost mortar joint. Installing the gap would have been quite diffi-cult given the shapes and dimensions of the short log pieces. Despite this minor "energy nosebleed" in the construction, the sauna has been easy to heat.

The snowblocking can be ordinary cordwood masonry, of course. We used the milled log pieces because they were available, quick to in-stall in the precisely defined space, and lent a little variety to the wall. Whatever snowblock material is chosen, it is infinitely easier to install before the roof goes on. At the Earthwood house, inclement autumn weather forced us to install the roof before the snowblocking, a much less efficient order of events.

The Roof Deck

The roof deck at the Earthwood sauna is octagonal and consists of eight facets of recycled spruce 2 × 6 tongue-and-groove silo boards, covered by a ⅜-inch chipboard. The boards span across each pie-shaped section between rafters.

Begin the planking at the outside edge, allowing a two-inch over-hang beyond the rafters, as in the photo on page 105. As the rafters themselves overhang the cordwood wall by 14 inches, the total roof overhang is about 16 inches at the points of the octagon, reducing to a 12-inch overhang at the midpoints of the octagon's edges where the walls curve out under the roof.

The first facet of planking is easy. Set the outermost board first and work your way in. Let the boards run a little past the centerline of each rafter and nail it with two nails at each end of the planks; just be care-ful to keep the nails well inside of the center of the 4-inch-wide rafters. Next, snap a chalkline on the planking directly over the centerline of each rafter. Set your circular saw to a depth just 1/16-inch deeper than the thickness of the planking, and cut both edges straight. The saw will just tickle the top of the rafters. When you are done you will have a nice pie-shaped facet of planking covering the rafter space.

4-11. Old silo boards are nailed to the wagon wheel framework.

4-12. The Bituthene membrane is installed over chipboard, which covers the planking.

The second facet requires a little more work. One end of each plank has to be cut with a 22½-degree angle (you can use an adjustable angle or speed square to mark the precise angle) before installing; as with the first facet, let the board run a bit long. After all the planks are nailed, snap a line over the rafter centerline to mark the ragged ends of the planking, then trim the facet clean with a single straight cut.

The final facet is the trickiest, but not to worry: you are now experienced in the vagaries of octagonal geometry. Whereas on the first seven facets you begin at the outside and make use of ever smaller pieces as you work toward the center, the last facet requires that you begin with the small piece at the center and work your way out, finishing with the longest piece on the outside edge. (If you start with the long piece first, it is impossible to fit the other boards in.) On this facet you will have to scribe both ends of each board with the 22½-degree angle. Nail them in and you are done with the planking.

Above the planking, nail down a layer of ⅜-inch chipboard and seal the joints between sheets with duct tape. There are two reasons for this. First, the chipboard provide a smoother surface for receiving the Bituthene membrane. Second, the 200-degree temperature near the roof of the sauna might melt the rubberized asphalt of the membrane and cause it to ooze its way down through the boards if nothing is beneath.

The Earth Roof

There is really nothing different about the earth roof on the round building. As with the Log End Sauna, you must install the drip edge, the Bituthene, an inch of extruded polystyrene insulation (which doubles as a protection board), the black plastic, crushed stone, hay or straw filtration mat, and, finally, the earth itself. Simply follow the instructions for the earth roof given in the previous chapter.

Originally, we held the earth on the sauna roof with heavy leftover barn beam pieces, fastened together on their top sides with truss plates. After about ten years, some of the old timbers were falling apart with rot, and we replaced them with the moss sods, as discussed on page 63.

The Eight-Sided Sawdust Concrete Floor

As reported earlier, the drain didn't work very well at first on our Earthwood sauna because it was at the same level as the rest of the floor. But we saved the day with a little creative forming and sawdust concrete.

First, I installed a 24-inch-long 2 × 4 spacer between the two 4 × 8 door jambs. This spacer provides a stop for the 24-inch-wide sauna door to close against, and retains the edge of the new sawdust concrete

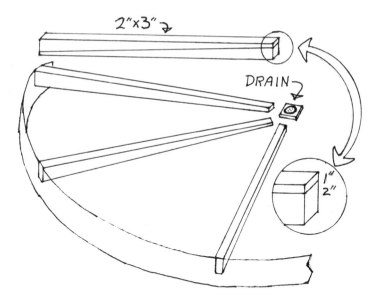

4-13. Eight 2 × 3-inch pieces were laid down on the flat concrete floor. (See also figure 4-14.) The eight pie-shaped pieces were then poured individually with sawdust concrete.

floor at the door location. The only slight drawback is that there is a 2-inch step up into the sauna, not really a problem. Next I ripped an eight-foot 2 × 6 down the middle and cut the resulting 2 × 3s in half, resulting in four 48-inch pieces of 2 × 3. Then I ripped these smaller pieces in half again, but on the bias as shown in figure 4-13. The eight pieces thus created each contain a one-inch slope when laid down on a flat slab, like our sauna floor.

I spaced these little forming boards on the concrete slab, one under each rafter for design symmetry, and nailed them down with masonry nails. Finally, I mixed and poured sawdust concrete into the eight pie-piece-shaped sections, as described in the previous chapter. At the center, the forming boards fell a few inches short of the cast iron drain, and I simply used a small trowel to feather all the concrete into a tidy little water-collecting depression. Now, the floor feels warm to the bare feet, due to sawdust concrete's low conductivity, and the water is carried away beautifully. In 1996, I painted the floor with a tan-colored acrylic concrete floor paint, and I am very pleased with the results. The floor looks better, is easier to sweep, and seems to drain better, too.

The drain (gray) water eventually comes out above grade some distance from the sauna. Check to see if this is acceptable under your local code. On small lots, a soakaway pit may be needed to receive the gray water. I don't advise draining to a septic tank, at least in the North. A trap would be necessary under the drain to stop odors from the tank, and then the trap would freeze solid in winter whenever the sauna is not in use. In the South, the septic tank might be a viable option.

Platforms in a Round Sauna

Installing platforms in a round sauna poses challenges not found with the rectilinear design. Some creative carpentry is needed, but nothing too outrageous. You can make use of the forming pieces left in the floor (as described above) for fastening one end of some 2 × 4 support posts. (The illustration below shows the location of platform support posts, and nailers.) The higher (42-inch) bench on the north side is made a little differently from the lower (36-inch) bench on the south side. In both cases, the supporting posts at the edge of the sauna are

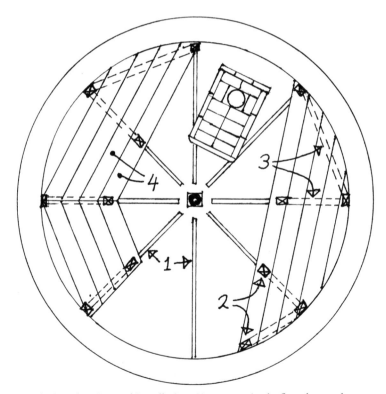

4-14. Platform location and installation. (1) 2 × 4s set in the floor slope to the center. (2) 2 × 4 posts. (3) 2 × 4 ledgers. (4) 2 × 6 platform planks, supported by ledgers.

stabilized by screwing them right to the cordwood walls. The 2 × 6 bench material itself stabilizes the five little 2 × 4 support beams (three for the high north platform, two for the south platform).

The ends of the bench planking are supported by ledgers fastened directly to the cordwood walls, as described in chapter three. These planks have to be carefully measured, scribed, and cut to match the curvature of the wall. All components of the platform—posts, little beams, and the bench planking itself—are made of eastern white cedar, which has proven to be a great choice. In 15 years, it has yet to stain. It has required no maintenance, except for a quick rinse with clean water at the conclusion of each bath. Again, remember to countersink screws or nails.

With leftover material, I made a heavy 12-inch-high sauna stool, the only piece of movable "furniture" in the bath; it's handy for accessing the high platforms and for placing the bucket upon during washdown. Sometimes, our son Darin, who still finds the top platforms kind of hot, uses it as his own private bench.

Windows

For windows in the Earthwood sauna we found two perfect 18 × 20-inch pieces of insulated glass at the local glass company. They were free, thrown in with some other inexpensive units we bought for the house. We mounted them in their own rough-cut two-by-eight frames, leaving a quarter inch of air around the insulated glass unit (as described in the previous chapter), and positioned them at eye level just under the plates on the south side of the sauna. As the door also has a small thermal pane window, the sauna has plenty of light and views during daytime bathing.

There are lots of special design features in the sauna, but they are best left for chapter six, devoted to that kind of neat stuff.

THE OVAL SAUNA

I conclude this chapter with a curved wall sauna I designed for an intentional community. They liked the "feel" of the curved wall stoveroom, but wanted to accommodate up to eight people. And, as the sauna would be a considerable distance from any house, a changing/relaxation room was included in the plan. Finally, the plan allows the wood heater to be fired from outside the stoveroom itself.

4-15. The Oval Sauna. Drawing by Jeremiah Lee.

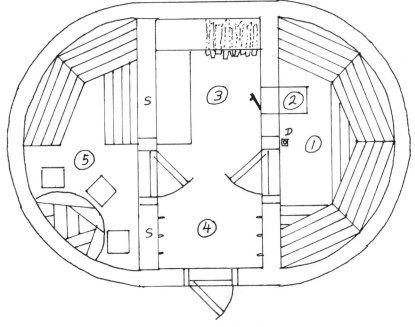

4-16. The Oval Sauna floor plan. See text, page 111.

Because the stoveroom is larger than other saunas described in this book (77 square feet usable), 12-inch cordwood walls are specified. The stoveroom and changing/relaxation room are the same size, each half of a 14-foot inside diameter circle (16 feet on diameter). The rectilinear entrance mudroom and woodstore has true inside dimensions of 6 by 14 feet. The internal wall next to the stoveroom is 12-inch cordwood, while the other internal wall is composed mostly of storage shelves, with just planks or boards on the mudroom/woodstore side. This floor plan works well for space, but can be altered to meet individual requirements. All three doors are 30 inches wide and must open out from the rooms. Window size and placement is a matter of individual taste and availability of recycled or bargain units, but no more than two small ones should be put in the stoveroom.

Here is the key for the floor plan illustration:

1. *Stoveroom.* The stoveroom has four 42-inch-high platforms and two smaller, lower (16-inch-high) platforms (which also serve as access steps to the upper levels). A couple of the high platforms could be installed a foot lower, if desired. D marks the location of the stoveroom drain.

2. *Heater.* The stone-covered heater is fired from the other side of the wall, so the stoveroom stays cleaner and combustion air is external. A good stove recommended for this sauna is the Nippa Model WC 22 woodburning heater with 12-inch firing extension, made by Bruce Manufacturing (see Appendix One). The heater is surrounded by 12-inch concrete blocks as shown in the photograph. This would be the view from the woodstore area.

3. *Woodstore and stove firing area.* Fuel wood is stored under 48-inch-high by 24-inch-wide shelves. Towels and other sauna supplies are stored above the shelves. Or, this can be a little kitchen area, if countertop is installed at 36 inches off the floor.

4. *Entrance and mudroom.* Boots, shoes, coats, and hats are stored here. There is room enough for a small fridge or icebox.

5. *Changing/relaxation room.* The floor plan is flexible. Relaxation benches, table, and chairs are all easy to fit. The long wall (S) in this room is planked on the mudroom side, with lots of 12-inch shelves and cubicles built in for change of clothes, stereo, snacks, drinks, etc.

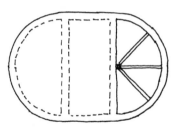

4-17. *A monolithic floating slab could be used for the entire building, or, as shown here, the stoveroom walls could be supported with a perimeter footing in the shape of a hemisphere. Sawdust floor facets could be poured later, sloped to a drain. Dotted lines indicate where the normally 3-inch slab is thickened to 8 inches at the edge of the building and for internal footings.*

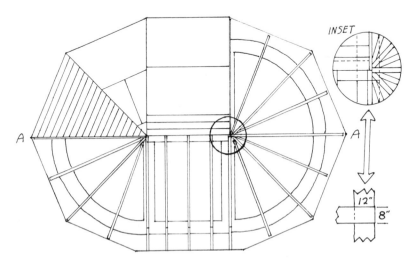

4-18. *Oval Sauna, structural diagram. Inner radius of hemispheres is 7 feet. With 12-inch cordwood walls, the outer radius is 8 feet. An 8 × 12-inch post is located at each of the two focal points, built in to the internal walls. These posts support an 8-foot long 8 × 8 girder, which, in turn, supports the parallel rafters. The 7-foot high 8 × 12 posts can be built up of 2 × 8s, 4 × 8s, or any convenient pieces. All rafters are 2 × 8. You'll need twenty-four of them, each about 10 feet long to accommodate the 16-inch overhang. Rafters over the rectangular room are 24 inches on center, except that the outermost parallel rafters are brought in an extra 3 inches to make room on the beam for the inner end of the radial rafters. Roofing can be 2 × 6 tongue-and-groove planking or 3/4-inch plywood.*

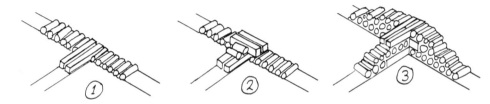

4-19 *Intersecting cordwood walls are knitted together with a modified "stackwall" corner.*

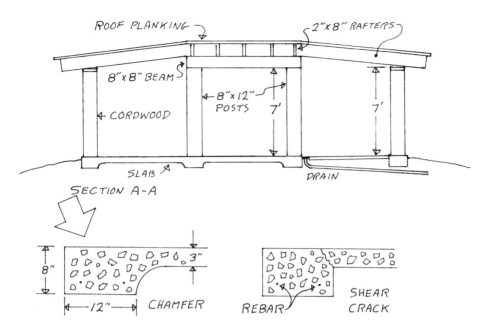

4-20 *Oval Sauna, Section A-A (see figure 4-18). This section shows the roof pitch (about 1:12), the two posts and the girder, the cordwood walls, the drain, and the floating slab foundation. As designed, the structure will support an 8-inch-thick earth roof, assuming red or white pine structural members, or equivalent. The slab is poured monolithically, 3 inches thick with footings thickened to 8 inches. See also figure 4-17. The stoveroom can have its four sections of sawdust concrete poured later, using wood dividers for the pie-shaped sections as shown. The combination slab and footings pour will require 4 cubic yards of concrete, so make sure a concrete truck can get to the site, or use some modification of the Shockey foundation, described at the end of chapter three. The inset shows the benefit of chamferring the edges of the footing pour. A shear crack might be avoided.*

With a concrete foundation, and new Nippa wood heater, and all new rough-cut framing lumber, my guess is that the Oval Sauna could be finished for a total outlay of $2,000 to $3,000, depending on the cost of doors, windows, and cordwood, and the builder's ability to scrounge recycled materials. Costs could be halved or better with a Shockey-type foundation, a homemade stove, and lots of recycled materials.

· 5 ·

The Sauna Stove

HEATING OPTIONS

Basically, the three fuel options for heating the sauna are wood, gas, and electricity. Stoves and heaters designed and manufactured for the purpose are available using all three fuel sources. Manufacturers, suppliers, and importers are listed in Appendix One. Other options include building your own wood-burning stove or adapting one for use in the sauna.

It is important to know at the design stage what kind of heater you will use. If gas or electric is required, connections must be planned for. Appropriate clearances from the heater to combustible material must be maintained, and different heaters have different clearance requirements.

Which heat source is best? I don't think there is any single right answer to this. The best choice depends on individual circumstances and considerations. Certainly, electric heaters are the most popular units in the U.S., and these are supplied with manufactured sauna rooms over 95 percent of the time. Real sauna nuts, particularly old-timers from Finland, favor wood as the only authentic heat source for a sauna. Gas heaters have not gained wide popularity, but may be the right choice where wood burning is restricted and electricity is not available. Let's take a closer look.

Electric Heat

Whatever you do, don't defeat the thermostat on an ordinary space heater, as I did in my young and foolish days. I'm lucky I didn't burn the cottage down.

Electric heaters are:

CONVENIENT. Flick a switch, wait a couple of hours, and you are ready to sweat. And the temperature can be thermostatically controlled.

CLEAN. No bout adoubt it.

SAFE. This assumes they are installed to code and manufacturers' specifications. Some units are wall- or corner-mounted and require virtually no clearance to the walls for safe operation. This can be a huge advantage where space is tight.

Disadvantages include:

EXPENSIVE TO INSTALL. Many manufacturers insist that their heaters be installed by licensed and bonded electricians, which is probably a good plan in any case, but it drives the cost up. Shop

5-1. Model WC wall/corner electric sauna heater by Amerec Products.

5-2. Electric floor-standing sauna heater from Finlandia Sauna.

around for the units. Prices vary tremendously. For the size and scale of cordwood masonry sauna described in this book (300 to 500 cubic feet), prices for an uninstalled heater with controls would range from about $400 to well over $1,000. Be sure to compare apples with apples.

EXPENSIVE TO RUN. A typical 8 kilowatt (8,000-watt) heater, which would be used for the size of saunas discussed in this book, might be on for four hours. (Remember that the massive cordwood sauna will take longer to "ripen" than the heavily insulated manufactured saunas that these heaters are designed for.) So 32 kilowatt-hours of electricity might be used. In rural areas of northern New York in 1996, electricity costs about 12 cents per kilowatt-hour, so one bath would cost $3.84, give or take a buck. Not bad for a party, but kind of costly for an individual. In fairness, I must report that one dealer I spoke with claims a much shorter burn time and a per-bath electricity cost of about a dollar. Yet another dealer insisted that an electrically fueled bath using his heater in his cabinet would cost considerably less than a dollar.

BORING. This is obviously a biased, opinionated, individual value judgment. I plead guilty . . . of being an incurable romantic. As clean and neat and tidy as electric units undeniably are, a part of me wants that live, temperamental, homey wood fire. I spoke with many a Finnish-American during research for this chapter, some with over 30 years in the sauna industry, and they were all adamant that the genuine sauna is wood-fired.

Gas Heaters

While not as common, natural and propane (LP) gas-fired sauna heaters have been available for a number of years. Their advantages include:

FLEXIBILITY. Gas heaters can be used in moderately remote sites where wood is either not available or where wood-burning is prohibited.

FAST. In general, gas heaters will get the stove room temp up to speed faster than wood or electric.

CHEAP TO RUN. Because of shorter heating times and propane's greater fuel-cost efficiency, gas-fired saunas are usually cheaper to run than electrically heated saunas.

5-3. Nippa model G-18 gas sauna stove by Bruce Manufacturing Company.

5-4. Finlander gas sauna heater by Finnish-American Sauna.

Disadvantages of gas-fired sauna heaters include:

LESS CHOICE. I could locate only four manufacturers of gas-fired sauna heaters, and only one—the Nippa—seemed to be within the parameters of affordability suggested by a cordwood masonry sauna. Most gas sauna heaters cost over $2000.

MORE DIFFICULT INSTALLATION. As with electric heaters, the gas heater should be professionally installed. Select a contractor experienced in gas appliance installations.

UNPOPULAR. Throughout the length and breadth of the land, I hear the same comments from suppliers: There is very little call for gas stoves. They don't seem to satisfy the convenience-oriented market, which favors electric, or the traditionalists, who favor wood stoves.

Wood Heat

Many hard-core saunees insist that only a wood-fired sauna is the genuine article. Most outdoor rural saunas are probably wood-fired. I admit to being partial toward wood heat myself, although I have enjoyed many a delightful sauna in electric-fired units.

5-5. Nippa model WC wood-burning sauna stove, with extension to allow firing from outside the stove-room, by Bruce Manufacturing Company.

5-6. Helo Sauna model 181/VS wood-burning sauna heater with water tank, from Saunatec, Inc.

Wood heat advantages include:

RENEWABLE. All wood comes from a renewable resource. In addition, scrap wood can be used effectively in the sauna stove as long as it is unpainted and untreated.

"AUTHENTIC" ATMOSPHERE. Many Finns maintain that there should be at least a hint of wood smoke in the stove room. Building the fire and keeping it stoked is part of the ritual.

INEXPENSIVE. Wood costs less than electric or gas, both for initial installation and in fuel costs, providing, of course, that wood is a locally available indigenous resource. This advantage may not hold true in the desert southwest, for example.

Disadvantages of wood heat include:

INCONVENIENCE. You have to cut, handle, and dry all that wood.

NOT AS CLEAN. Ashes need to be emptied out of the stove. Wood bark, sawdust, and dirt can make the stoveroom untidy.

SAFETY CONSIDERATIONS. A safe stovepipe must penetrate the roof. Many wood heaters, particularly homemade ones, may require a lot more clearance to walls than, say, electric heaters do.

KONNOS (THE ROCKS)

No matter what fuel source you choose, an important consideration in selecting a stove will be the quality of the heat produced. A heater should have the ability to transfer strong radiant heat into "softer" conducted and convected heat. This transfer is normally accomplished by insulation in or on the sides of the heater and a good supply of "konnos" (sauna rocks) on top of the heater. The rocks are heated to high temperature by whatever fuel is used, and then give the heat off into the room in a more gentle manner. Oh, the stones are hot all right. Make no mistake, like touching them. But they have the ability to heat the atmosphere, and the fabric of the stove room itself, less harshly than a stove, which relies on high-level radiant heat. The heat from the konnos is said to be softer, not cooler. The rocks act as a buffer. And they are critically important to the creation of the löyly, the shot of steam that returns the sauna to its ancient origins.

Before the advent of enclosed stoves, the heating chamber, or *kiuas*, was typically a pile of rocks with a fireplace or pit in the middle. Remember the savusauna, or "smoke sauna?" The wood fire heated the rocks to very high temperatures, the smoke was vented out of the room, and the konnos provided all the heat as well as the facility for creating

5-7. An early version of the savusauna kiuas.

löyly. The heating of the North American Indian sweat lodge is accomplished in much the same way, even today, although sometimes the rocks are heated outside the chamber and then brought in.

While stove design and safety have improved a great deal in the past 100 years, the goal is the same: soft, high-temperature heat and good löyly. The best stoves, still called kiuas today by the Finns, are those that provide this desired atmosphere.

While not the only consideration in a purchasing decision, the amount and type of rocks used are very important. Almost all the Scandinavian heater manufacturers supply their own imported rocks with their units, usually dolerite, peridotite, basalt, or other igneous rocks. This strikes me as a sales gimmick. Perfectly good rocks are available, of course, in North America. There is a huge basalt (traprock) quarry, for example, just 10 miles from my home.

Manufacturers also seem to delight in telling why the way that they heat the rocks is best. Some offer deep wells of rocks, others spread them across the top of the heater. Certainly, the total weight of the rocks is important, and this can vary from just 25 pounds to over 200 pounds. Other considerations being equal, I tend to favor the models with greater rock storage capacity. Thermal mass is one area where bigger can, in fact, be better. Size-wise, most authorities recommend stones about the size of a softball, grapefruit, or clenched fist.

STOVE CAPACITY

Manufactured units are generally matched to stoverooms of certain sizes, measured in the United States in cubic feet. I have no reason to think that cordwood masonry saunas will perform any differently from insulated manufactured sauna cabinets sheathed with ¾-inch boards, except that the cordwood sauna will take longer to heat because of the much greater mass. On the other hand, it will also store the heat longer without additional heat input. So I would stay with the manufacturer's recommendations concerning the cubic foot capacity of their various models, even with the cordwood sauna.

For nonrated or homemade units, you can use the following rough guidelines for determining capacity: For electric heaters, allow 1 kilowatt (Kw) for every 55 cubic feet of stoveroom. With gas, figure 1,000 BTUs of rated output for each 15 cubic feet of stoveroom capacity. The cubic capacity of a wood firebox should be about 1.5 to 2 percent that of the stoveroom.

Another consideration for any kind of stove, especially homemade, is burn protection. Many stoves are sold with wooden guardrail protection.

INSTALLATION OF ELECTRIC HEATERS

Your job is to know which of the many commercially available heaters you want for your sauna, so that you can allow the required space and clearance. Send for manufacturers' information and specifications, or visit the nearest showroom (the manufacturers or distibutors will tell you where that is). Now your job is done. Installation of a high-output electric sauna heater is not a job for the weekend warrior, unless said warrior happens to be a licensed electrician.

The manufacturers don't want you to install their heaters, either. There are many sound reasons for this. First, the circuits required for the heavy electrical draw are typically 240-volt single phase or 208-volt or 240-volt three-phase circuits, a couple of degrees of difficulty over, say, adding a 120-volt plug to an existing line. In our area, 208-volt three-phase power is only available for commercial accounts. And, because water and electricity don't mix (and you will sometimes be standing on a wet floor), the entire installation must have ground-fault interrupted (GFI) protection. This is normally accomplished by use of an expensive GFI circuit breaker back at the breaker box or a GFI protected receptacle. These devices sense a "ground fault" (such as your naked body completing a circuit to ground) and trip the breaker so quickly that you don't even feel the slightest shock. Once, when we lived in Scotland, Jaki was filling an electric kettle that was plugged into a 240-volt receptacle. She became an integral part of that circuit and describes the experience as akin to being hit hard across the back with a two-by-four plank. Our circuits were not ground-fault protected.

In addition, all wiring and electrical equipment must be outside the stoveroom, including the control panel, thermostats, and all other junction boxes . . . even the light switch. Electric light fixtures should be of the "vapor-sealed" variety, commonly available for bathroom use. With an outside sauna, all conductors must be in conduit buried 24 inches below ground. An electrical inspection by a certified inspector is not only a code requirement, but gives you safety protection and peace of mind. I think you can see why it is best to leave it all up to a licensed electrician.

GAS SAUNA HEATER INSTALLATION

I have come across four designated gas sauna heaters, though there may be others. All are capable of running off of liquid propane (LP) or natural gas. One style, made in two sizes by Vico Industries of South Elmonte, California, and sold by Cedarbrook Sauna and Steam (see Appendix One), makes use of a direct-vent system through the wall. Combustion air comes in, and the exhaust goes out, through the same triple-walled direct vent, much like a propane-fueled wall furnace. No additional vent or chimney is required. Vico makes a 40,000 BTU model for an 8-foot by 11-foot stoveroom, and an 80,000 BTU model for huge commercial saunas up to 12 by 20 feet. These heaters carry a 10-year warranty, typical in the industry, but, according to John Lysaker of Cedarbrook, they cost about $2,000 more, installed, than a comparable electric model. Cedarbrook sells them to Alaska hunting camps where there is no electricity, and to large commercial saunas in places where electricity is expensive.

Another type of gas heater, the Nippa made by Bruce Manufacturing Inc. of Bruce Crossing, Michigan (see Appendix One), seems more appropriate for an outdoor family sauna. They cost about a thousand dollars, comparable to electric sauna heaters, and are installed similarly to wood-fired models; that is, they require an air intake vent and a Class A chimney flue to remove the exhaust. Like other gas-fired units, they require no electricity whatsoever, which makes them a good choice if the sauna is some distance from the house. According to Bruce Manufacturing owner Gil Kotila, the sauna heats faster with gas than with electric heat. Gil says that Bruce sells a lot of gas sauna heaters to people living in areas where wood burning is restricted. Such "clean air" regulations are becoming ever more common. Bruce Manufacturing supplies safe gas (and wood-burning) sauna stove installation specifications.

While chimney connections may be accomplished by an owner-builder (as described in the wood stove installation section that follows), I strongly advise that all gas connections be made by a licensed contractor experienced in gas appliance installation. Most gas suppliers have skilled installers on their staff. All gas connections must be tested for leaks before the heater is used.

UL Listing

The sauna heaters manufactured by the larger American manufacturers, as well as most of the heaters imported from Scandinavia (such as Helo, Tylo, Finlandia, and others) are "UL-listed." This means that Underwriters Laboratories, an independent testing lab, has tested the appliance and found it to be safe for its intended purpose. A UL listing does not mean that other manufacturers are putting out an unsafe or inferior product. It requires much money and time for a small manufacturer to have its product UL-listed, and, in many cases, these costs just don't pay for themselves in terms of greater sales. I called my insurance agent to ask if homeowners' insurance underwriters are insisting upon UL-listed products. He says that they are not, and that regardless of whether a particular heater was UL-listed, an insurance company might still sue the manufacturer if the cause of a fire was found to be a fault in the heater. In his many years of experience , my agent has insured a lot of saunas, and can remember only one claim, the result of owner negligence. He says that whether or not a heater is UL-listed "isn't a big deal," and won't become a big deal unless sauna claims become a major problem—something unlikely to occur in the U.S., where comparitively few saunas are in service.

Manufacturers or importers who have invested a lot of money in gaining UL approval will use the listing as a selling point, even advising avoidance of non–UL-listed products. Check with your insurance agent before making a purchasing decision based substantially on UL approval. My homemade sauna stove is not UL-listed, but our sauna is still covered under my homeowner's insurance. Incidentally, a CSA listing (Canadian Standards Association) can be considered to be substantially equivalent to UL. I have even been told that CSA tests are more stringent.

WOOD STOVE PLANNING
AND INSTALLATION

Several manufacturers, domestic and foreign, provide wood-burning sauna heaters, usually called stoves. Many are made in Finland, where they are in common use. Unless restricted by regulation, wood heating probably makes the most sense for a free-standing outdoor sauna.

Stove specifications vary widely. Many, like the Saunatec, made in Finland, have insulated walls, which enable safe placement of the stove to within 8 inches of combustible walls. The sauna is heated by the rocks on the top of the stove, in the traditional manner, rather than by heat escaping from the sides of the stove. Other stoves are made of heavy-gauge steel and have less wall insulation. Strictly speaking, according to the NFPA (National Fire Prevention Association, which publishes standards upon which building codes are based), uninsulated stoves should be 36 inches from any combustible wall, and ordinary single-wall stovepipes at least 18 inches away. These are the extremes of clearances, from minimum to maximum, depending on the kind of stove. Appendix One lists some of the manufacturers and distributors of wood-burning sauna stoves.

With a family-sized sauna like the ones described in the previous two chapters, stove clearance can be a major concern. Luckily, with the use of stove protection boards or 16-gauge sheet metal mounted 1 inch off the wall, the 36-inch clearance from walls is reduced to 12 inches, and the 18-inch stovepipe clearance is reduced to 6 inches. Decorative fireproof wall and floor protection panels come in a variety of sizes and colors, including brick and stone motifs. Any such wall protection should be kept an inch from the wall by the use of a spacer, such as a 1-inch porcelain electric fence insulator. Remember that many if not most designated sauna wood stoves do have sidewall insulation and, therefore, can be installed closer to walls. Go by the manufacturer's specifications.

Bruce Manufacturing produces Nippa wood-fired sauna stoves "hand-crafted since 1930 in Michigan's rugged Upper Peninsula." All Nippa sauna stoves have an optional 6-inch, 8-inch, or 12-inch firing extension for feeding the stove from outside or from an adjacent dressing room. Installation specifications supplied by Bruce Manufacturing show the firing extension built into an 8-inch concrete block wall. Such a 40-inch high block wall, near the stove, would be compatible with an 8-inch cordwood wall. Simply fill the block cores of the top course with concrete and begin building with cordwood directly above this top course. A four- or five-course block wall near the back and sides of a woodstove could eliminate the need for the protection board in situations where space is at a premium. Firing the stove from an adjacent changing or relaxation room gives more room in the stoveroom, and is safer and cleaner.

Clearance above any type of sauna stove should be at least 36 inches. Maintaining such a clearance will not normally present a problem, as sauna ceilings are typically seven feet (84 inches) high and stoves are never more than three feet (36 inches) high (even to the top of the rocks), so a 48-inch overhead clearance is guaranteed.

Stovepipe Installation

Stovepipes are potentially more of a fire hazard than the stove itself. As a housing inspector, I used to observe many situations where home-owners had given their stoves plenty of clearance, but ran the stovepipe within 6 inches of a wall or ceiling. A stovepipe gets cherry red during a 1,900-degree chimney fire, while a stove might not.

Fortunately, sauna stoves are normally burned hot, preventing creosote from forming inside the stovepipe. Creosote comes from un-burned wood gasses that condense on the inside of a cool stovepipe. A hot fire, such as a paper or kindling fire, can cause this hard or sticky black substance to ignite. Chimney fires burn houses down in New York's North Country all too frequently in the wintertime.

For fifteen years, the stovepipe at the Earthwood sauna exited the rear of the stove, which forced the stove close to the center of the room. In 1996, we gained a lot of floor space by moving the 6-inch-di-ameter stove exit piece to the top of the stove. At the same time, I sur-rounded all sides of the stove (except the front door panel) with bricks, some 300 pounds of mass in all. Previously, only the top surface of the stove was so covered. The bricks, which absorb the direct radiation

5-8. The Earthwood sauna stove was converted to top exiting and surrounded with 320 pounds of bricks, changes which allowed us to place the stove closer to the wall and increase the useful floor space.

and convert it to a more gentle, convected heat, allowed me to place the stove much closer to the cordwood walls, about 9 inches now. We gained much more washing space, while improving access to the platforms.

I have never been an advocate of exiting a wall with a stovepipe. The extra elbow, in combination with the horizontal run and the extra stovepipe in the cold outside, tends to create more creosote than with an installation that exits the ceiling. As soon as possible after exiting the stove, the pipe should be converted to "Type A" chimney, such as a triple-walled pipe or one of the lined pipes such as Metalbestos stovepipe. The Metalbestos type is expensive at a little over $3 per vertical inch for the parts (in 1996, so that my 6-foot-high chimney, for example, would cost about $225 now). Yet it is the system I prefer. I have installed at least ten Metalbestos chimneys, and I find the system easy to work with, visually attractive, and extremely safe. There is no asbestos in Metalbestos, by the way. The pipe consists of an inner and outer layer of stainless steel separated by an inch of dense, inert, mineral fiber insulation. The pipe is UL-listed as safe within 2 inches of combustible material.

Here are six tips that can save you hundreds of dollars in purchasing Metalbestos chimney.

1. Ask your dealer (generally a hardware or stove store) if he or she has any imperfect sections you could buy at discount. Sometimes sections get slightly dented in transport, for example, and can't be used for an expensive installation where the appearance is highly important, as in a living room. I have often bought such sections for half price or even less.

2. Ask for a discount on perfect pieces. There is a high mark-up on Metalbestos, and it certainly doesn't hurt to ask.

3. Check with local contractors. Sometimes they remove class A chimneys as a part of a home renovation, and they might be willing to sell them at bargain prices.

4. Watch the classified ads and local Pennysaver-type advertising papers. I have often seen Metalbestos chimney sections advertised quite inexpensively.

5. Watch garage and lawn sales. Again, I have seen many a section go for a song and a dance. Check all such "bargains" for real damage. Particularly, make sure that the insulation isn't spilling out, and that the sections lock properly one to the

other. Obviously, do not mix sizes. There is no way to join a 6-inch- to an 8-inch-diameter section.

6. Use 6-inch chimney, not 8-inch. It is much less expensive, and I have not encountered a sauna stove requiring a chimney larger than 6 inches. (Best check your stove specifications just to be sure, however.)

Installation of the Metalbestos chimney is not difficult for someone who is even moderately handy. At the two earth-roofed saunas I have built, the procedure was the same. Installation takes place as soon as the waterproofing membrane has been installed.

1. From inside the stoveroom, drill a small locating hole up through the planking, corresponding to the center of the stovepipe.

2. On the roof, and using your locating hole as the center, describe a circle with a 6-inch radius (12-inch diameter) on the membrane. Why a 12-inch circle? Well, 6-inch i.d. (inside diameter) Metalbestos actually has an 8-inch outside diameter, because of its inch-thick walls. Then you need to allow 2 inches all around the pipe to meet the UL listed rating for the chimney: 8 + 2 + 2 = 12.

3. Cut the 12-inch hole through the roof, using either a recipro-

5-9. The entire Metalbestos chimney is supported by the "ears" of the Roof Support Package.

cating saw or (I have to admit I've done it) a chainsaw. I recommend the reciprocating saw.

4. The first piece of pipe to install is the RSP, or "Roof Support
   Package." This part is a regular piece of Metalbestos pipe having two adjustable angle-iron ears, one on each side of the
   pipe. The ears, positioned with the roof slope, are lag-screwed
   to the roof deck. The RSP is then made perfectly plumb with
   the two adjusting screws on the ear. I use the plumb bubble of
   a four-foot level to get this right.

5. Next install the pieces between the stove and the RSP. Stovepipe pieces in the stoveroom are locked into the RSP piece
   hanging through the ceiling by applying an upward pressure
   with a slight rotational twist. Special locking bands are used
   to more positively join one section to another, particularly
   with the hanging sections. An RSP will easily support 10 feet
   of Metalbestos pipe. Chimney pieces come in a variety of
   lengths, ranging from 6 to 36 inches, so it should be possible
   for the ordinary stovepipe leaving the stove to change over to
   Metalbestos almost immediately.

6. Install adequate chimney above the RSP (outside). For a sauna
   stove that is normally burned hot and fast, I have found that
   48 inches of chimney extending above the RSP is plenty. Check
   local code, however, as some areas require a taller clearance.

*5-10. The flashing cone is sealed to the waterproofing membrane with strips of
Bituthene, caulked along the edges.*

7. Next, I install the flashing cone that comes with the Metalbestos system. Flashing cones are made for flat roofs, for roofs
of 1:12 to 6:12 pitch, and for roof pitches greater than 6:12. I
have most often used the 1:12 to 6:12 style. This aluminum
cone fits down over the chimney and is nailed to the deck right
through the waterproofing membrane. Sometimes I have
used ribbed aluminum nails having a little round neoprene
washer just under the head. Such a nail compresses the washer
as it is driven home, creating a waterproof seal. Even so, for
insurance, I still apply a 6-inch strip of Bituthene along the
edge of the flat flange portion of the flashing cone — 3 inches
lapping onto the flange and 3 inches onto the existing
Bituthene membrane. On some applications, I have just used
ordinary galvanized roofing nails every three inches, then covered the nails with the 6-inch strip of Bituthene. Caulk all cut
edges of the Bituthene with a compatible caulking and feather
the bead of caulking with a pointing knife. This stops the edge
of the membrane from lifting or "fishmouthing."

8. Install a "storm collar" just above the top of the flashing cone.
This diverts rain water away from the top of the cone. I always
caulk the top of the storm collar with a bead of clear silicone
caulking.

*5-11. Drainage is the better part of waterproofing! Chimneys must be surrounded
by good drainage detailing. Here, the stovepipe and flashing project through a wood
frame filled with crushed stones. Water running down the chimney is carried
quickly to the 2-inch-thick crushed stone drainage layer described on page 63.*

9. Finally, install a chimney cover, or "round top," on the top section. This attractively designed piece finishes the top of the chimney esthetically and stops rain from running down the inside of the pipe.

A HOMEMADE SAUNA STOVE

I designed the stoves for both Log End Sauna and the Earthwood Sauna. Both work well, but the Earthwood design has a little more capacity, is slightly easier to build (because all angles are right angles), and is a little easier on which to install bricks on the top and sides. Igneous rocks, such as basalt (also known as "traprock") are great for the top of the stove, but might be difficult to hang on the sides unless enclosed in some sort of wire mesh support.

As it is difficult to insulate the sides of a homemade stove with double- or triple-wall construction, I strongly recommend the use of bricks on the outsides of the side walls. The bricks transfer the stove heat from a high-intensity radiant heat to a low-level conducted and convected heat, much like the rocks already discussed. Without the bricks or stones, the bather cannot comfortably hang his or her legs over the edge of the platform near the stove. The direct radiant heat from the stove is simply too strong. I use bricks called "red matt solids." It is not

5-12. The stove at Log End Sauna is made from 1/4-inch plate steel, but has a slightly different design (and less capacity) than the Earthwood sauna stove plan described on the next page.

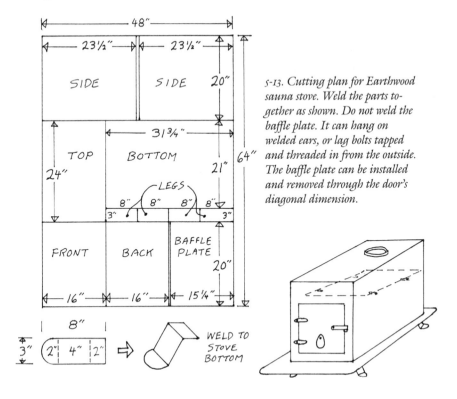

s-13. Cutting plan for Earthwood sauna stove. Weld the parts together as shown. Do not weld the baffle plate. It can hang on welded ears, or lag bolts tapped and threaded in from the outside. The baffle plate can be installed and removed through the door's diagonal dimension.

necessary to use more expensive firebricks, although I expect they would work quite well if the opportunity to recycle a pile of them happens to come your way.

All of the parts for the stove can be cut from a 4-foot by 5-foot, 4-inch (48-inch by 64-inch) piece of ¼-inch plate steel, bought at a metal shop. Many metal shops will cut the parts for you. Just bring them a copy of the cutting plan shown above. They might even weld the stove for you. Or, you can take the parts and the plan to a welder and have it assembled, as in the illustration. Perhaps a local farmer or garage mechanic can do the welding. Perhaps you are a welder yourself.

For fifteen years, we used the Earthwood sauna stove without the baffle plate and without the bricks on the side. I had always meant to make those improvements, which were a part of the Log End Sauna stove. Finally, inspired by writing this book, I performed the retrofits, which has made the sauna easier to heat and the platforms more comfortable for sitting. The sauna is hotter, yet the heat is definitely softer.

I did not use the full 21-inch-wide by 31¾-inch-long base section shown in the plan, which incorporates a 2½-inch shelf around the edge of the stove for easy placement of bricks. Instead, I had to bolt sections of angle iron on the bottom of the stove. The reader might as well get it right the first time. A 5-inch shelf catches ash or hot coals just below the door.

The baffle plate is an important part of the design, and I have wasted a lot of fuel over the years because I didn't install it earlier. The baffle creates a secondary combustion chamber above the main part of the firebox. The exhaust is forced to travel along the underside of the baffle plate and to enter the secondary combustion chamber near the front of the stove. Then these hot flue gasses (commonly known as smoke) enter the very hot top chamber, where they are ignited. This second burn increases the efficiency of the wood by up to 35 percent and decreases pollution and the potential for creosote formation. The hotter firebox temperatures (increased fuel efficiency) translate to a higher temperature of the fabric of the building itself, particularly the inner surface of the log-ends and the inner mortar joints.

Now, with the retrofit, we have 300 pounds of dense red bricks surrounding the firebox. These bricks grace the performance of the stove in two ways: (1) Although the stove actually burns hotter, the heat is "kinder and gentler," to borrow a phrase. The harsh radiant heat that burned knees, shins, and feet when the side of the stove was bare iron is converted to a softer convected heat. The walls and platform planks close to the stove do not get nearly as hot as they used to, yet the thermal mass of the sauna taken as a whole is definitely warmer. (2) The 300-plus pounds of bricks stores heat much longer than the 120-odd pounds which we used to have just on the stove top. The sauna stays hot much longer between firings, fully twice as long. A full day after my initial test of the new stove retrofit in mid-February, the stove room was still warm despite 0 degree temperatures outside and very strong winds.

Adapting a Stove for Sauna Use

Many readers may find that recycling an old woodstove for sauna use costs even less than making one's own from scratch. Lots of sound old cast iron and plate steel stoves can be found at garage sales, discount stores, and in the classified ads. There might be one sitting out in the barn that will do the job. I would use cast iron if I could be sure that water would be poured only on hot stones or bricks for making steam, and never directly on the iron, which could crack under the thermal shock. I would avoid thin-walled sheet-metal stoves and stoves made from 30- or 55-gallon drums. These could be dangerous in the stove room.

Although appearance is not all that important in a sauna stove, structural condition is. Stoves can be smartened up remarkably with a wire brush, stove black, and plenty of elbow grease. Cracks in cast iron, however, are virtually impossible to repair, so a cracked stove should be rejected out of hand. Look for a stove that can easily accommodate bricks or stones on the sides and top. The importance of this thermal mass surrounding the stove cannot be overemphasized. An old pot-belly stove, for example, might look like just the thing for the job, but unless it is internally lined with firebrick, the radiant heat might make the bather rather uncomfortable. In general, a stove with straight sides will work best. A fireplace insert stove, surrounded with bricks, might also fit the bill nicely, though it will take a little more planning to accommodate its width. Some stoves have both end and side loading options. Perhaps the side doors can be covered with bricks in some way, and all the loading can take place through the narrow end door.

When it comes to safe installation, I tend to be a bit more conservative. If the budget is tight, try to find some Class A chimney using one of the six cost-saving suggestions listed above. I have seen many a creative system of penetrating a wall or a ceiling with a home-made insulated pipe. I am sure that some of these have been well thought-out and are probably safe, but, frankly, most of them have scared me rigid.

COMBUSTION AIR

A fire cannot burn without oxygen. People can't breathe very well without it, either. For both reasons, a sauna heated with wood needs a source of fresh air, or *combustion air*, so the stove won't use up all the oxygen in the room.

At the Earthwood Sauna, a 3-inch pipe in the first course of cordwood masonry supplies combustion air to the stove. It seems to work well, although I would use a 4- to 6-inch-diameter pipe if I were doing it again. We have not found it necessary to conect this pipe positively to an air inlet on the stove, but the closer the inlet pipe is to the firebox, the better the air supply. A larger pipe size gives more options.

Without a good source of outside air, the stove won't run well and will try to rob air from the interior of the sauna, causing an oxygen shortage. Ventilation is one of the most important components of a pleasant sauna experience. Some experts, including V. S. Choslowsky, executive director of the Sauna Society of America, and Erkki Lindstrom, known as "the Sauna Man," have personally advised me that ventilation is *the* most important consideration. I figure you can always decrease the diameter of an air inlet pipe, but it's not easy to remove a log-end in a cordwood wall to increase ventilation. I do have two 8-inch-diameter vents further up the wall, each having removable log-ends to allow the regulation of air flow. Their purpose is to provide extra fresh air to the bathers, as needed, and their construction is described in the next chapter. And by the way, cordwood masonry walls "breathe" better than most, promoting natural and frequent air changes. This is one reason that I am not in favor of sealing off one or both sides of the wall.

I have seen many diagrams supplied by the manufacturers of sauna rooms showing "ideal" ventilation patterns, but they don't always agree. And so many outside influences can affect the "ideal" patterns: shape of the room, type and placement of the stove, trees, topography, orientation, and so on. My advice is to give yourself plenty of venting options, and then, by trial and error, find the pattern that works best for your sauna. These options include the several different wall vents described in this book, the inlet pipe at floor level for combustion air, various roof or ceiling vents, and the old standby trick of cutting an inch off the bottom of the door.

Stephen Larsen's wood-stove in his round cordwood sauna is fired from the outside. It does not take any of the sauna air for combustion. I like this idea.

5-14. The Larsen sauna. A meditation room, being added to the top, will provide overhang protection for the cordwood wall. This photo and overleaf by Merlin Larsen.

· 6 ·

Variations on the Theme

A T I T S H I G H E S T level, the sauna takes on an almost spiritual characteristic, akin to the Japanese tea ceremony. In the way that a
religious architect designs a church to bring the parishioners closer to
God, so should the sauna room's fabric be in harmony with the sense
of well-being—and sense of fun—found within its walls.

CORDWOOD MASONRY
DESIGN FEATURES

Building a cordwood wall has much in common with the sculptor's
art. Materials are molded, shaped, and placed by hand to achieve a
particular goal. On the face of things, this goal would appear to be the
simple construction of vertical walls. But, as words can be shaped and
combined into lyrical verse, log-ends and mortar can be shaped and
combined into visual poetry: pleasing designs, harmonizing textures,
shadows and color.

Texture

The texture of a cordwood wall is a combination of the surface characteristics of the log-ends with the amount of relief between wood and
mortar. With many woods, a pleasing and interesting pattern emerges
from the end-grain if the log-ends are sanded or wire-brushed. Test the
wood before you build with it to find out what beauty might be

hidden within. (Always use eye and nose protection. Fine cedar saw-dust, in particular, is really nasty in the lungs. I've coughed for hours after working without a face mask, and I'm sure the stuff doesn't do the body any long-term good either.)

My favorite tool for brightening and beautifying an interior cord-wood wall is my Makita 4,500 rpm 5-inch disk sander (see figure 2–1). The most convenient time to sand the log-ends is just after the wall is built. This gives the added benefit of cleaning any mortar that might be left on the surface of the logs. If the builder is certain that he will want to sand the log-ends later, he should be careful to leave the ends proud of the mortar background by at least a quarter inch. Remember to leave the interior ends of the logs in the same plane for reasons cited in chapter two: comfort of the bather and ease of fastening platform ledgers. Taking care in log placement also makes the sanding process much easier to perform. The interior of a small building like a sauna can be sanded in a few hours with a good disk sander. If you don't have one, hire one for a day from your local tool rental store. And buy plenty of disks; the store will usually take the unused disks back. I find that a medium grit works best, combining speed with smoothness.

A rotating wire brush can also do a remarkable job, and, depending on the wood species, can create a particular texture a disk sander can't. Wood grows fast in summer and slow in winter, so each annual growth ring is composed of hard and soft layers. A wire brush wears the soft parts of the rings more than the hard parts, leaving a sandblasted look. (Sandblasting? Never tried it. It would probably be great.) If power tools are not feasible at the site, a plain buck-ninety-eight wire brush—in combination with elbow grease—does an admirable job.

A fast log prep that can be done prior to construction is to give the log-ends a quick buffing on the rotating wire brush end of a bench grinder. Again, wear eye and nose protection. And keep your fingers out of the grinder.

As discussed in chapter two, there is little point in sanding or brush-ing the exterior of the sauna. Let it weather naturally.

Pattern

My favorite cordwood masonry "pattern" is no pattern at all—what I call the "random rubble" look. This lack of pattern helps use all the dif-ferent sizes and shapes of log-ends at a fairly constant rate. If because of unusual procurement circumstances you happen to have log-ends all the same size, they can be quickly and easily laid up in courses, every

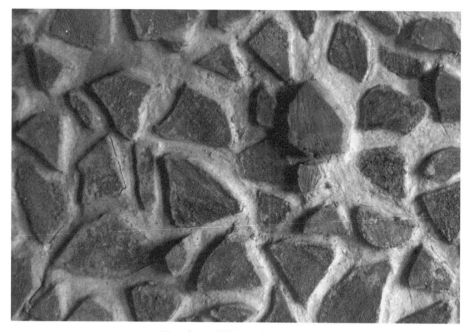

6-1. "Random rubble" cordwood masonry.

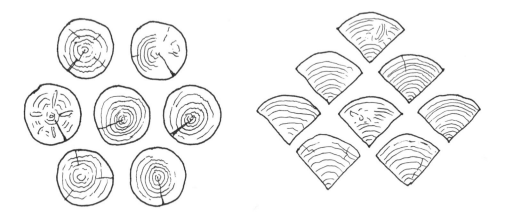

6-2. Left: If all log-ends are about the same size, courses can be laid up quickly, producing a hexagonal pattern. Right: Quartered log-ends can produce their own pattern. Let the epidermal layers of the wood shed rain water away. Don't do this one upside down.

other course offset by half a unit. With round logs, the net effect will be a hexagonal or honeycomb configuration. With quartered logs all the same size, a similar pattern can be employed, as in the illustration.

6-3. This pattern, employed on a house in Parson, British Columbia, made use of two sizes of log-end. The large pieces came from a fencepost maker, the small pieces are all 3 1/2-inch diameter peeler cores from a plywood plant.

Special Design Features

Whatever the predominant masonry style selected—random rubble, hexagonal configuration, you name it—special designs, log-ends, shelves, bottle-ends, and the like can be incorporated into the wall. Within a regular pattern, the design features will jump out at the viewer as a departure from the norm. With the random rubble style, the design might have to be accented in some way, such as leaving the featured log-ends even more "proud" of the mortar than usual. The special log-ends are cut an inch longer than the others, two inches if the design pattern is desired on both sides of the wall. Another accenting trick is to sand the featured logs while leaving the rest unsanded. I have adapted both techniques, sometimes in combination.

MEDITATION POINTS. "You need a meditation point in this sauna," said Ken Gable, one of my students at a cordwood masonry workshop. "What's that?" I asked. "It's got to have seven elements," said Ken, not quite answering in kind, but I suppose it was a pretty dumb question anyway. "Elements? Like what?" "Have you got any special log-ends, something with a little energy in them?" asked

Ken. I replied that I had brought back a few red cedar log-ends left over from Sam Felts's beautiful cordwood home in Georgia. "Perfect," said Ken, "They'll have good energy." We mortared seven of Sam's log-ends together at eye-level, a hexagon with the seventh log-end in the center. I polished the ends with my sander, which freshened their aromatic quality. Thus, we combined the meditation point with another cordwood custom which I call the Adam's Rib concept: A log-end is taken from one project and installed in someone else's home or sauna. Thus, some of the energy of the first project is transplanted to the second. Cordwood aficionados do this all the time.

And what is a meditation point? Well, it has to have seven elements . . .

DIVAS AND MUSHROOMS. Another student at the same workshop, Ed Burke, spent most of his hands-on time creating little design features in the cordwood masonry. He was having a ball and doing a good job, so we let him go his merry way. Next to the door, Ed made a replica of the Hindu good luck symbol, the reversed swastika, using four consecutive log-ends taken from an old split cedar fence rail, each having the cross-section of the first-quarter moon. At the exterior lower right corner of this design, Ed created

6-4. Ed Burke's creativity appears just outside the door at the Earthwood Sauna.

a Diva to protect the sauna from evil spirits, such as "Bannik," the evil Sauna Spirit. We had some mystics at that workshop, but they weren't all quite so cerebral; one student included Pacman chasing power pellets.

Ed Burke also included an apple design on the interior, and portraits of Rob and Jaki on the exterior. Jaki is the smiling figure on the right of the picture, Rob is the crank at the upper left. Ed's Diva and portraits were accomplished by careful pointing and small colored pebbles for facial features.

Jaki and I put a lot of cordwood mushrooms in the wall. I don't know why. We just like mushrooms and they're easy to do, particularly with white cedar log-ends and pieces cut from old split cedar fence rails, my favorite cordwood building material. Their creation is self-explanatory, as seen in the photos below. Butterflies are easy, too. We take a long log-end of roughly triangular cross-section, cut it in half, and open it up like a Rorschach ink-blot pattern. Larger triangles form the upper part of the wings, smaller triangles the lower parts.

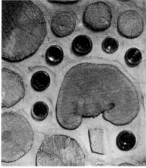

6-5. (top left) Rob and Jaki.

6-6. (left) Mushroom.

6-7. (above) Rorschach's Butterfly.

Giant Log-Ends

For several years, I had been keeping an eye on a huge log in the back lot of the local sawmill where I do business. The log was almost eight feet long and about four feet in diameter. The species is rather romantically called "balm of Gilead" (*Populus candicans*), a cottonwood variety quite similar to balsam poplar. I knew that Ron Marx, the owner of the mill and a friend for several years, had found that the behemoth was too big to mill into lumber. To prevent rot and insect damage, I had taken it upon myself to remove the very thick bark from the log. And there it sat. One of my fantasies was to someday slice the log into huge log-ends, and feature them in a cordwood wall. The result would be the Machu Picchu of cordwood masonry.

Finally, at the Earthwood Guest House, the opportunity to use the log presented itself. I bought a quantity of cedar from Ron Marx for a raised bed garden project, and said, "Look, Ron, you're never going to use that balm of Gilead log. Why not throw it on the truck and tidy up your yard?" He did. I came home one day to find the thing off to the side of our driveway. Oval in shape, it measured 52 inches in diameter across the long axis, 46 inches the shorter way. I hired a 48-inch Stihl chainsaw to slice 9½-inch-thick disks off the log, much as you slice a carrot or banana. Even so, the saw wouldn't quite make it all the way through the log, and I would have to move from one side of the log to

6-8. The author cuts 9-1/2-inch disks from a 52-inch-diameter balm of Gilead log.

the other a few times to make each cut. The saw was sharp, however, and the cut stayed straight, so the surfaces of the log-ends are flat and smooth, with very little evidence of the saw cut.

Even though the "log-ends" were only 9½ inches thick, they weighed, by estimate, over 300 pounds apiece. How would we move them and lift them onto the cordwood masonry? And even if we could get them into place, what would stop these megaliths from crushing the wall? Moving them turned out to be fairly easy. Son Rohan and I simply reinvented the wheel and rolled them the hundred yards to the site. But it was apparent that we would not be able to lift the huge disks. Luckily, we didn't have to. I made a cradle for each giant log-end out of pressure-treated 2 × 6 lumber scraps.

First, every 4 inches along both edges of the 2 × 6 scraps, we set roofing nails, leaving the heads protruding about a half-inch. Later, these nails would help tie the scraps to the mortar. Then, with masonry nails, I fastened the longest scraps directly to the concrete foundation, centered both with regard to the width of the foundation, and the length of the 53 by 72-inch panels in which the disks would be featured.

Rohan and I then rolled, pried, and generally manhandled the disks onto these pressure-treated pieces. It took a while to get them centered in the panels. Then, using a wedge-shaped, full-length cedar log-end as a jammer, we completed the cradle by tightening a short piece of the pressure-treated material against the balm of Gilead, one each side, as shown in the photo below.

6-9. A pressure-treated 2 × 6 plank keeps the giant off the concrete slab. A wedge-shaped cedar log-end is driven in to steady the big guy. Roofing nails help grab the mortar to come.

The final consideration was to make sure that the big log-end was in the same plane as the panel itself. We used the plumb bubble of a four-foot level, but also eyeballed from the corner posts to the center post. Temporary diagonal bracing helped to hold the 300-pounders in place while we built around them with ordinary cordwood masonry. The pressure-treated cradle, of course, is now completely hidden from view in the portion of the wall normally reserved for sawdust insulation. The roofing nails have done a great job in keeping the mortar from vibrating loose and breaking away from the panel.

Each giant log-end makes up exactly half the area of the panel in which it appears, the other 50-odd log-ends and mortar accounting for the rest of the panel. Viewed from either the interior or exterior, the balm of Gilead giants add tremendous character and interest to the sidewalls of the Guest House. While not quite as impressive as Machu Picchu, the Guest House giants do provoke the same kind of head-shaking wonder.

6-10. The rest of the cordwood panel is built around the giant log-end.

Artistic Pointing

A few years ago, I conducted a cordwood masonry workshop at the Center for Symbolic Studies in New Paltz, New York. The workshop project was a 12-foot-diameter round sauna with 10-inch-thick walls, about 25 percent bigger than the Earthwood Sauna. Obviously, an institute involved with myth and symbolism draws a lot of very creative types to a workshop, but two of the most creative were codirector Robin Larsen and her son, Merlin (who had practiced at an earlier workshop at Earthwood). Robin, Merlin, and their friends and students incorporated a number of mythical figures and designs, mostly by the use of creative raised pointing techniques. Dragons, goddesses, and spirits all appear on both interior and exterior wall surfaces. Bits of broken mirror, marbles, and special stones were used to advantage in many of the designs. Yours truly was responsible for several shelves

6-11. (above) Earth goddess at Larsen's sauna.

6-12. (top right) This sauna matron . . .

6-13. (right) . . . stayed in a little too long.

All photos by Merlin Larsen.

and bottle-end designs, discussed a little later in this chapter. All told, the Center's sauna is an amazing compendium of designs, many of them subtly hidden.

Tom Johnson and Tim Miller in *The Sauna Book* advocate a certain amount of artistic license, but also caution: "If the walls are too busy, you will be surrounded by the very stimuli you are trying to escape." While the saunee may be distracted for a few minutes by dragons and goddesses, the initial stimuli is soon replaced by a quiet spiritual enjoyment, much as is experienced by looking at a familiar view or a stained-glass window in a church.

Bottle Ends

Speaking of stained-glass, the cordwood equivalent is the use of "bottle ends." Ever since we built Log End Cottage, over 20 years ago, Jaki and I have incorporated colored glass designs in cordwood masonry walls. When the sun—or even artificial light—hits the bottle-end design, the effect is nothing less than spectacular. It's as if each individual bottle end has a 25-watt bulb glowing inside. Designs can be random or patterned. Even elaborate panels—the Phoenix rising out of the ashes, for example—can be created. For maximum effect, place the bottle ends on the western wall, preferably away from a window, as the glare can drown out the desired effect. A morning person (not me) might choose the east wall. Bottle ends on the south wall are only so-so in summer, when the sun is high, but catch the winter's low rays fairly well.

At the Cottage, with its 9-inch walls, we actually went to the trouble of cutting two bottles with a bottle cutter and gluing them together with epoxy, eliminating the necks altogether. This technique was only moderately successful, and required a lot of work. A few of these glued bottle ends took on a little moisture somehow, and, when subjected to heat from direct sunlight, actually cracked from heat expansion. They would certainly fail in a hot steamy sauna. By the time we built Earthwood, in 1980, we had developed a new technique which has been 100 percent successful; that is to say, we have installed hundreds of bottle ends without a single one breaking.

Here's how: Select two bottles (or jars, or a bottle and a jar) and plug each of them into a cylinder made from a piece of aluminum printing plate enclosed in a couple of stout elastic bands. Printing plates can be obtained wherever offset printing is done. The plates are used only once. Some printers throw them out, some will give them away, and some—like our local paper—sell them (for 40¢ apiece around here). Ask and you will receive. The best rubber bands are the ones the Post Office uses to fasten bundles of bulk mail envelopes together. If you are well-known at your post office—not with your picture on the wall—they will probably give you a bag of rubber bands.

The key is selecting bottles and jars that, when fitted together, make a bottle end about the same length as your standard log-end, or even up to an inch longer. With a 10-inch bottle end in a 9-inch wall, for example, the bottle end can be an extra half-inch proud on each side of the wall. I mention this as an option, because it can be difficult, sometimes, to find two pieces that are only 9 inches long when fitted together. Recently, at the Earthwood Guest House (with its 9-inch walls), we included about 50 bottle ends in the various panels. We had the most success combining a beer or iced tea bottle with a clear jar of the same diameter. It is important that the diameters of the two halves of each bottle end be the same. If they are very much different, the "spring-loaded" aluminum cylinder doesn't work too well. It tends to spit out the large bottle or jar.

With a razor blade knife, cut the tiny folded edge off the printing plate; these edges, used by the printing machines to hold the plates in place, make it difficult to roll the plates into cylinders. Then, figure out the size of rectangle that will work best for the required cylinders. For 10-inch bottle ends, I cut rectangular pieces 5½ or 6 inches wide, which allows the mortar to bond to about 2 inches of glass at each end. (Mortar bonds chemically to clean glass.) As for the rectangle's length, 10 inches is sufficient to wrap the typical 2½-inch-diameter beer bottle. A 12-inch length will be necessary for wider jars. I can usually get 12 rectangles of aluminum out of a standard 22 by 30-inch newspaper plate.

Once you have cut your pieces, simply roll the thin-gauge aluminum rectangle into a cylinder and "spring load" it with two hefty elastic bands. Plug the glass in from each end until the bottle end is the required length. Often, this will mean that the bottle and the jar will actually touch each other; the top of a longneck beer bottle will bottom out in a salsa jar at about 9½ inches.

In most cases, with a relatively narrow sauna wall, a bottle is best married to a clear jar. When the bottle end is laid up in the wall just like any other log-end, the clear end—the jar—is placed to the exterior, so that the vibrant colors of the bottle are accented on the interior. If the colored end is placed to the outside, the color is very much diffused and not nearly so attractive. Brown and green beer bottles work well, as do certain blue mineral water bottles. The ginseng-flavored Arizona Iced Tea comes in a beautiful cobalt blue bottle, and the tea's not bad, either. Sometimes we put two 4½- or 5-inch jars together to make a clear bottle end. With sauna walls, a lot of jars will be needed. The best source in our part of the world is at the recycling bin of the county landfill.

The aluminum cylinder is a vital part of the bottle end "unit." Without it, the sawdust insulation will greatly diminish the amount of light transferred through. With 16-inch walls, as at the Earthwood house, we simply plug two 8-inch bottles into the cylinder, usually one clear and one colored bottle. The use of two colored bottles tends to cut way back on the amount of light that gets through.

The bottle ends should be placed in the wall carefully to maximize the esthetic effect. I look for balance and the same kind of planned randomness that I use with the log-ends. Sometimes I will make a deliberate diamond or hex pattern (the old "meditation point").

If an elaborate bottle end panel is desired, do a "dry run" first on a flat piece of plywood the same size as the intended panel. Michelangelo might have called the plywood his "cartoon." Place the bottle ends and log-ends on this cartoon, allowing proper space (about an inch) for mortar joints. This dry run on a horizontal surface makes planning an elaborate design much easier. Now, one at a time, transfer the masonry units from the cartoon to the actual panel in the wall. Neat, huh?

People always ask, "What about heat loss with bottle ends?" Sure, there is some heat loss, but not a lot. The glass does not directly conduct all the way through the wall, so—on a per-square-inch basis—the loss is no more than that of insulated glass. As the average bottle end has about five square inches of cross-sectional area, it would take 72 bottle ends to equal the heat loss of just one of our little 18 by 20-inch sauna windows. Very little comfort is lost for style here.

Shelves and Towel Pegs

Little shelves can be handy for holding matches, toiletries, whatever. They can be made from either half-round log-ends cut a few inches longer than the width of the wall (a 16-inch log-end for a 10-inch wall, for example) or a full round log can be cut half-way through as shown on page 150, and then split with a hammer and wedge. The rough shelf

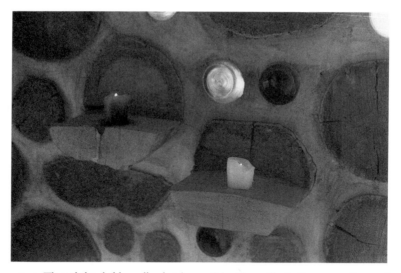

6-14. These shelves hold candles, but be careful with candles in the sauna: they tend to melt!

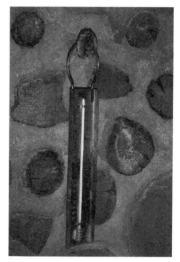

top can be sanded smooth with a disk sander. Put the shelf where it's handy, but out of the bathers' way. If it doesn't work out, it can always be sawed off. Shelves might be particularly handy in the changing or relaxation room.

Although undressing really shouldn't take place in the stoveroom, a few pegs by the door are handy for hanging towels, the thermometer, the whisks, the loofah sponge, the ladle, and so on. Simply lay up a very small (⅝-inch) log-end cut about 3 inches longer than the width of the wall. I have also used old railroad spikes for clothes hooks.

6-15. The thermometer hangs from a railway spike.

Dowels can also be used as pegs by drilling the appropriate sized hole right into a log-end and driving the dowel into said hole. For hanging towels, drill the hole with a slight downward angle.

Air Vents

I like to put a few air vents in the stoveroom, at about head level. We put four in at Log End Sauna, two at the Earthwood Sauna, using a different technique at each location.

At Log End, we wrapped 6-inch-diameter cylindrical log-ends with ⅛-inch corrugated cardboard, and mortared the unit in place in the normal way, except that the mortar joint against the cardboard went continuously through the wall; the sawdust insulation was left out at this one location. After the mortar was hard, we tapped out the cylindrical log-end with a hammer and peeled the corrugated cardboard away from the mortar. Simply put a little wooden knob handle on the log-end and you can remove and reinstall it easily as needed. It will fit almost perfectly.

At Earthwood I used a slightly different technique. At about eye level, I mortared up a 10-inch-long by 8-inch-diameter ceramic "thimble" into the wall like a log-end. (These thimbles are used to join a stovepipe to a masonry chimney, and are readily available at a masonry supply yard.) The thimble provides the vent opening; now the trick is to find a round log-end of 8-inch diameter to fit the hole. Once you find one, put a little wooden handle on the log-end, and the vent is ready to use. (I actually wrapped a little weatherstripping around the log-end to give an almost airtight fit.) At Earthwood, I placed the two 8-inch-diameter vents almost directly opposite each other, one a few

6-16. This log-end plugs the ceramic thimble vent.

inches higher than the other in order to promote a good cross-draft. (Warm air rises.)

We find that removing the log-ends, particularly one on each side of the room, can provide bathers, especially neophytes, with a welcome breath of fresh cool air. They can also serve as windows for views in directions not served by other windows.

THE SAUNA CABIN

This chapter deals with fun and fantasy and dreams, so it's a good place to talk about the ultimate in sauna pleasure and comfort, The Sauna Cabin. More than a sauna, this design could actually serve as a complete vacation retreat: one-room cabin, sauna, and bathroom. The large room could serve as changing room, relaxation room, bedroom, kitchen, and dining room, all rolled into one.

The cabin is built using the post-and-beam method. The plan, which is fairly self-explanatory, shows suggested locations for corner and sidewall posts.

The "Temporary Shelter Strategy"

Many people own land in the country on which they intend to build a house someday. Perhaps they visit the property once in a while, even camp there for a few days at a time. They are fortunate to have one of the major requirements needed for building a house: the land. The other major requirements are money and building experience. Here, the Sauna Cabin can come to the rescue, and in a most enjoyable way.

Shelter is the single most expensive part of living costs in North America. The temporary shelter strategy can actually eliminate shelter costs in six months to a year, enabling the owner-builder to save money at a greatly increased rate. The strategy, in short, is to build a small temporary shelter—the Sauna Cabin!—and live in it while you build your house, thus saving continued shelter cost. You also gain valuable building experience, particularly if you adopt the same construction methods later on the home. After building the Sauna Cabin, you won't want to build your home any other way. The old saw—"Experience is the best teacher"—certainly cuts the wood when it comes to cordwood masonry. Think of it this way: better to make a $500 mistake on the temporary shelter than a $5,000 mistake on the main house later on.

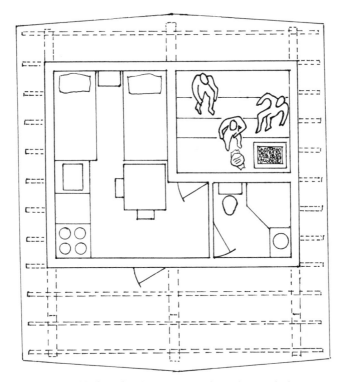

6-17. One possible floor plan for a Sauna Cabin. The outside dimensions of the cordwood walls are 14 feet by 16 feet. Rafters are 24 inches on center.

Although I speak of a temporary shelter, the Sauna Cabin is by no means a temporary structure. It is simply a place to "tough it out" for a year or two while an individual or young family builds a home. Notice we have come full circle to the long-successful strategy of the Finns, both in the old country and in the new: build the sauna first, and live in it while building the house. When the main house is finished, you will still have the Sauna Cabin, which can then double as a guest house.

At the other end of the economic scale, some readers may wish to adapt the Sauna Cabin as a luxury retreat. Still others may see the design as a hunting cabin.

Internal Walls

The internal stoveroom walls could be cordwood, or they could be well-insulated 2 × 6 framed walls with a vapor barrier on the warm side of the insulation. The stoveroom panels can be made of any of the woods discussed earlier as suitable for the platforms. Make sure that the boards are really dry, though. Some so-called "kiln-dried" wood from the lumberyard still has a 15 to 20 percent moisture content. Ideally, the wood should have less than 10 percent moisture content, which it will be soon enough at sauna heat. If you start with 18 percent stuff, considerable shrinking will leave unpleasant gaps between the boards. Tongues will pop out of grooves. My suggestion is to lay up the boards horizontally behind removable (screwed) battens. After a year of saunas, the boards can be tightened up and permanently fastened; there should be no more noticable shrinkage.

Framed internal walls have some advantages over cordwood: They can accommodate wiring more easily (although surface-mounted wiremold is an option with cordwood). They can be drywalled and painted white, which will brighten the cabin a great deal. (Cordwood masonry is light absorbing.) They are somewhat faster to build.

If cordwood walls are selected for the interior, be very careful to maintain that sawdust insulated cavity throughout the wall. The insulation prevents the living quarters from heating up too much while the sauna is fired. If, despite insulation, too much heat is still passing from the stoveroom to the main room through the log-ends themselves (remember, cordwood breathes), install an inch of rigid foam on the

6-18. Sauna Cabin in Finland, made of horizontal logs. Photo supplied by Erkki.

relaxation room side, covered with drywall, tape, spackle, and white paint. It is probably a good idea to allow room for the insulation and drywall layers, just in case they are needed. If the cabin is primarily for winter use, such as a ski lodge, don't worry. The internal cordwood wall will act as mass heat storage. The small building can be heated simply by leaving the stoveroom door open.

The floating slab and earth roof techniques already described are equally appropriate to the Sauna Cabin. Our house, Earthwood, is a large 2,000-square-foot two-story house and makes use of both of these constructions methods. The floor plan suggested is just that: a suggestion. The scope of this book is really to build a small cordwood sauna, not a small house, but there are some components special to the sauna function which need to be discussed.

The Changing Room

A dressing room should be, at the minimum, the same size as the stoveroom, as with the oval sauna design described at the end of chapter four. After all, the same number of people are going to use it. Small stoveroom, small changing room. Large stoveroom, larger changing room. The changing room should include benches to sit on; it's hard to remove one's shoes from a standing position. It should include plenty of clothes pegs, spaced about 10 inches apart from one another. Hooks or double hooks work well, too. It may be useful to mount an attractive varnished board to the wall for the fastening of pegs or hooks, although this is not necessary on a cordwood wall. Remember to angle wooden pegs up slightly so that they hold the clothes better.

A series of shelves, like a linen closet without the door, are a very attractive feature in a changing room. They serve as a place for you or your guests to store clean clothes for after-sauna use. Towels and other supplies can also be kept there.

If the dressing room floor is likely to get wet, either from snow being tracked in from outside or water from the stoveroom, duckboards are advised. Duckboards are a series of small planks nailed or screwed to backing boards running in the opposite direction, much as wooden pallets are constructed. (Some people actually use wooden pallets, available for nothing or next to nothing from many local industries, such as building supply yards or newspapers. Make sure they are in good condition and that the boards aren't too widely spaced.) The duckboards should be made so that they are easy to lean against an internal wall; that way, both the floor and the duckboards themselves can dry easily.

Relaxation Room (or Cooling Area)

After a sauna, the cooldown process is important, as we will see in the next chapter. In the summer, or in the South, this is pleasantly accomplished on a deck or patio. In northern winters, however, you will need an inside relaxation area. Where the sauna is close to the house, as at Earthwood, a room in the house serves extremely well. But if the entire sauna is to take place in a remote spot, the relaxation room must be incorporated into the plans.

A relaxation room can be as simple or as elaborate as you wish . . . and can afford. In the Sauna Cabin plan, it can be the "great room," what the British call the "bed-sit." At minimum, it must have places for bathers to lie or sit comfortably. Wooden benches will serve well here just as they do in the stoveroom. In the relaxation room, saunees will be stretching out on their towels, which improves comfort somewhat, but it is a nice gesture to supply a few head pillows.

Cooling Tank

I have only once partaken of the cooling dip after a sauna, thirty years ago in Iceland. I remember that it was not nearly the shock to my system that I had expected, and that the experience was invigorating. I have also enjoyed a similar sensation on occasion by falling back into a fluffy snowbank. During research and many conversations with sauna old-timers from across the country (many of them, not so surprisingly, Finns) I am advised that I am missing out on the complete sauna experience by not having the cool dip option readily available. In light of that, I am considering putting in an outdoor tank close to the Earthwood sauna. I am also considering building a new sauna out at the Mushwood Cottage, just a short mad dash from the lake. Here is what I have gleaned from reading other folks' commentary on cool pools.

Johnson and Miller, in *The Sauna Book*, say that the width and length of the tank are more important than the depth. "Coming out of the stoveroom in full sweat, you shouldn't have to enter the cold water with delicacy and restraint. The only way to get in the tank is totally and with determination."

An unheated hot tub or spa will do, but these are expensive and you will probably want to keep them up to hot-tubbing temperature. We like saunas and we like hot tubs, but they are totally different experiences.

One of the best options for a cooling tank is a galvanized metal stock tank, available from farm supply stores. These come in a variety of shapes and sizes, but the long "oval" ones seem to be best for the purpose. In March of 1996, a new stock tank measuring 30 inches wide by 6 feet long by 2 feet deep cost $94.95. The tank holds 180 gallons and has a threaded drain plug at the bottom, which could be replaced with a hose bib for easy draining, an important feature. (A siphon hose will work, but it is not nearly as handy.) A simple cover for the tank is also recommended, to keep it clean and free of kids and pets. Unless you want to run a pool filter, the tank will have to be cleaned and emptied after every bath or two in summer, because of algae growth. In the winter, it may last longer because of cold temperatures, but if left unattended for a few days in sub-zero conditions, a cold tank can become a frozen tank and, finally, a hopelessly ruptured tank.

Speaking of pool filters, one of the least expensive cool tank solutions is a small above-ground backyard pool or large wading pool. A small pool can be kept clean with a filtration unit, while a large wading pool is a lesser investment but needs to have the water changed much more frequently. Bargains are available from the usual sources: yard and garage sales, classified ads, and Pennysaver-type ad sheets.

Finally, an old clawfoot bathtub can make an attractive cooling pool; it requires little water and is easy to plumb for draining. The downside is that the tub must be entered rather more gingerly because of its smaller size. The plunge won't be quite as dramatic as with the 180-gallon stock tank.

As cold water is what is required for a cooling pool, any of the tank options discussed in this section can be filled with an ordinary hose.

Well, everything's in place. It's time to sauna.

· 7 ·

Taking a Sauna

A CRYING SHAME

I T'S A CRYING SHAME that sauna has been misused in America," Erkki Lindstrom told me. The Sauna Man's concern was echoed by Vince Paladino, the savusauna advocate from BHS Sauna and Steam, and reechoed by several Finns involved in the sauna industry across North America. Some of these experts, many with 30-plus years of sauna experience behind them, sell electric sauna heaters because that is what most Americans want, while they themselves "chill out" in wood-fired baths.

Where have Americans gone wrong? Well, for openers, the word "sauna" itself has been stretched so far that the original meaning has been all but lost. For example, many Americans still think of a sauna as a steam room, a Turkish bath. Others, equally wrongly, think a sauna is an absolutely dry atmosphere with no steam—löyly—at all. I was guilty of this misconception myself for many years.

While writing this chapter I happened to stay at a Holiday Inn in Montreal, where I gravitated straight to the "sauna." The room was kept at about 145 degrees Fahrenheit and was absolutely dry, with no means available to the bather to increase either the temperature or the humidity. Although the electric heater had rocks on top, a wall sign proclaimed: "Do not pour water on the rocks. This is a dry sauna and moisture may damage the electric unit." The electric unit, of course, was designed to accommodate water and steam, but the hotel was having none of it. It was impossible to experience sauna there. I was disappointed and ended up in the hot tub, which was properly maintained. A Finn would have laughed, cried, cursed, or simply walked away in disgust.

THE FINNISH TRADITION

A tradition that lasts 1,000 years or more must have something going for it. Although the recipe for enjoying a sauna may have changed somewhat over the last millenium, the change has been slow, and, in general, has probably been change for the better, at least healthwise. The sauna ritual, as practiced in Finland, is now highly refined, yet not dogmatic as in Germany, for example, where exact prescribed times are allocated for each phase of the bath: how long to sit, how long to lie down, how many times to go in and out, and so on.

Finnish Architect Elmar Badermann says:

> In Finland, and perhaps in other countries, too, every sauna fan is convinced that his and only his is the right way to use the sauna. This is particularly the case with owners of self-built saunas. After all, who would be willing to concede that his own sauna was too dry, too wet, uncomfortable or unhygienic?

I plead guilty as charged, both with regard to the building itself and the way I use it. I like my sauna better than all others, but I know it is not really the best, as I am still able to make improvements to it, and I continue to refine my methods and patterns of use. Not surprisingly, the closer I get to the Finnish tradition, the better my sauna becomes.

The authentic Finnish sauna includes the following elements: Preparation, Perspiration, Löyly, Whisking, Cooling, Washing, Relaxation. Some of these elements may be repeated a number of times. There should be no hard and fast rules, unless it is this one: Leave yourself plenty of time. In fact, it is probably a good idea to put your watch away and unplug the phone. Your internal clock is the one to pay attention to.

First Curing

Your sauna is Finnished and you can't wait to fire it up and enjoy the fruits of your handiwork. Don't be hasty. There are a few considerations to attend to prior to that first firing, considerations that might not ever come into play again.

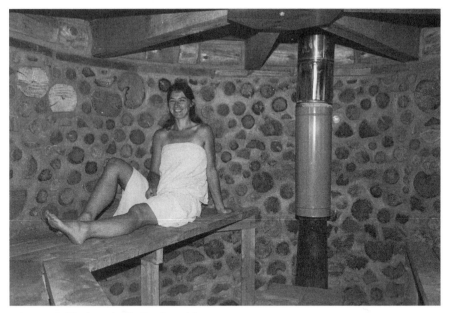

7-1. Jaki relaxes in the Earthwood Sauna.

CURING THE MASONRY. With a cordwood sauna, allow one full week after the last mud is laid before firing the stove. That soaked sawdust was put in the mix for a very important purpose: to retard the mortar set, which reduces mortar shrinkage and cracking. Premature high temperatures could cause cracks to form between log-ends.

FIRST CLEANING. After the mud has cured, construction dust should be removed. If you intend to sand or brush the log-ends, now is the time. After the dust settles, brush the walls, ceiling, and floor with a stiff whisk broom or plastic-bristled scrub brush. Pick up the worst of the dirt with a dustpan, wait an hour or two for airborne dust to settle, then vacuum the whole place top to bottom, including the tops and undersides of the benches and the heater or stove. Wipe the benches and any other smooth surfaces with a damp cloth. Wash the sauna rocks, if they have been unprotected, to remove construction dust.

FIRST BURN. Now, if your heater is a new manufactured unit, no matter what the fuel source, burn it for a good half hour with the sauna door and all vents wide open. This goes for newly welded or blackened woodstoves, as well. New heaters almost always have oil on the electric elements, or stove black, or protective coatings, or other industrial crud that produces a most unsaunalike aroma. Recently, I put an aluminum printing plate on top of my plate steel stove top (but under the bricks) in order to stop water from hitting the iron stove top directly. It took the best part of an hour to burn and dissipate the printer's ink. None of this is nice stuff to breathe.

Once the toxic fumes are completely gone, shut the sauna door and any major vents and bring the stoveroom up to temperature.

Ripening the Sauna

After the building has been cured and cleaned, the stoveroom must be ripened (sometimes called "seasoned") prior to use. This takes a while, particularly with a massive cordwood sauna, so a bath should be planned a few hours in advance, two at the minimum. This is part of the ritual and contributes to a sense of anticipation. Elmar Badermann writes:

> Any person who rushes into the ready-heated sauna directly after coming from work will leave it only half as relaxed as the person who has correctly lit the oven in the wood-fired sauna, collected the fresh birch twigs for the birch whisk and in those ways inhaled a little smoke and forest air. Heating the sauna by pressing a button, or even by dialing a number on the telephone, may save the harrassed executive some time, but will hardly reduce his burden of stress.

I can't tell you exactly how long it is going to take to ripen your sauna for use. It depends on the size of the room, the stove, the quality of the firewood, and, of course, the outside temperature and wind conditions. What I can tell you is what to look for in a properly seasoned sauna:

First, the interior fabric of the building should be up to temperature. Both the log-ends and the mortar joints should feel warm to the touch. If the masonry is cold, even though the air is hot, the sauna is not ready. Continued and frequent stoking of the wood fire will be necessary, because the thermal mass of the walls will continue to rob heat from the air. If the authentic smoky aroma is desired, now is the time to create it (see Fragrance on page 165).

In addition, the rocks (or bricks, in our case) must be very hot, so that they will vaporize water almost instantly.

Once the fabric of the building is warm to the touch, the fire can tick along slowly and keep the bricks or rocks hot enough to maintain the required air temperature. The Earthwood and Log End saunas, which have stoverooms of similar size, take at least three hours to ripen on a cold winter's day, two hours in the summer. High winds can add an extra half hour.

Temperature

And what is the right temperature? Dr. Ilkka Vuori, in an article called "Healthy and Unhealthy Sauna Bathing," says, "For most of us, a suitable temperature is between 70 degrees and 90 degrees C. (158–194 degrees F.) as measured at the eye level of a sitting person. In roomy saunas, the preferred temperature is about 10 degrees C. higher and in small saunas about 10 degrees C. lower than the figures above." This translates to Fahrenheit temperatures of up to 212 degrees (boiling temperature) in large saunas, and as low as 140 degrees in a small sauna. Personally, I find Dr. Vuori's temperature guidelines to be right on, except that I would also add age as a criterion. Thirty years ago, I preferred a sauna at about 20 degrees F. hotter than I do now, and all of my middle-aged sauna mates report the same phenomenon.

Sometimes, the Roy family will enter the sauna at about 140 to 145 degrees (remember children prefer lower temperatures, too) and we'll let it heat up to about 165 degrees. On other occasions, we might enter at the higher temperature and Darin, 10, will occupy a stool down on the floor. The two main platforms have a 6-inch height differential (42 and 36 inches respectively), which translates to about a 6-degree F. temperature difference, roughly 1 degree per inch of height. Jaki likes the lower bench and I prefer the upper. If I sauna alone and want to stay in a little longer, I'll stretch out on the lower platform.

Perspiration

The idea is to sweat. The main concept of this chapter can be expressed in those five words. Perspiration drives dirt, old oils, and sebum out of the pores from within, making the sauna one of the best, if not *the* best method, of cleansing the skin.

H. J. Viherjuuri tells us that "during perspiration, the prone position is preferable, because it enables the body to receive equal heat all over." As the feet and lower legs don't perspire as much, some saunas include a dowel extending from the upper wall placed to serve as a heel or leg support. With some platform designs you can incorporate a 2 × 4 rail into the design for propping up the feet close to the stove. Even a loop of cloth hanging from the ceiling will do the trick. Viherjuuri advocates this elevation of the feet: "The whole body should benefit from the heat." I do it as a matter of comfort and have not experienced the slightest hint of blood settling to my head, probably because blood movement throughout the body is accelerated during sauna.

The great heat of the sauna attacks the outer skin first. The body has two means of trying to maintain that ideal healthy temperature of 98.6 degrees F. It pumps extra blood to the skin to release heat, and the pores open to let the body perspire. The evaporation of this sweat normally causes a cooling sensation. In sauna, this is all a losing battle. The heart pumps faster, akin to a light aerobic workout, and we sweat more profusely. On average, adults sweat over two pounds of water (about a quart) per person per hour in sauna. Our mass temperature rises a degree or two over time.

Normally, the humidity in the stoveroom is very low at the beginning of the bath, typically 5 to 10 percent. As we begin to perspire, the water tends to evaporate quite rapidly into the dry atmosphere. After a few minutes, though, the sweat is running like so many tiny leaks in a membrane (a fair comparison) and our skin gets soaking wet. Puddles form on the platform planks, and then on the floor.

Löyly

It is at this point, when you have begun to sweat, that one of the main differences between the Finnish and the American attitudes toward sauna manifests itself. The Finns suddenly increase the humidity in the stoveroom by ladling a cup or so of warm or hot water onto the konnos, the rocks. The sacred löyly is created. Few Americans do this.

Instead, North Americans tend to maintain a dry climate throughout the bath, thinking, I suppose, that the lower humidity will make the sauna's high temperatures easier to endure. It is only recently that I have adopted the Finnish pattern of pouring water on the bricks that envelope the Earthwood sauna stove. Oh, we used to make a little token steam on request, but lately I have been bringing the bricks up to a much higher temperature, thanks to the new baffle plate in the stove, and the löyly created definitely has the characteristics described by Finnish advocates: It is nearly instant, its magic passing across the room in an invisible wave. It causes a pleasant tingling sensation as it hits the skin. It produces the sensation of being very hot, although it is probably about the same temperature as the air through which it travels. (The humidity makes it seem hotter.) It is deep penetrating, so much so that it seems to scour the nose, the lungs, even the soul.

In any wooden sauna, the porous walls absorb the löyly quite quickly, returning the atmosphere to near the starting humidity within a minute or two. Cordwood walls, with about 40 percent mortar and 60 percent log-ends on end grain, perform similarly to other saunas in this respect. Steam rooms, of course, have nonporous walls, usually shiny tile, and maintain the steam steadily throughout the bath, albeit at a necessarily lower temperature.

The sauna is a place of contrasts: warming and cooling, dry air and humidity. It is at the moments of transition between these contrasts that the sauna experience is most intense and stimulating. Sauna bathers who do not "take the löyly" are missing out. I know.

How frequently to add water to the rocks is a matter of individual taste, tempered by concern for one's fellow bathers. It is inconsiderate behavior to make the sauna unpleasant for anyone. Different temperatures can be experienced at different platform heights, but löyly pervades the entire stoveroom. If you like more and hotter steam than others, why not wait until they step outside for a cooling spell before ladling on the water?

A practical consideration is to use hot water to create the löyly, not cold. Water at higher temperatures vaporizes more quickly and completely, and has less cooling impact on the rocks.

Fragrance

Old-timers insist that the fragrance of wood smoke should be present in the sauna, not the smoke itself. This is probably a throwback to the glory days of the savusauna. Assuming wood-fired heat, the best way to achieve this wood smoke fragrance is to visit the stoveroom ten to fifteen minutes prior to bath time, close the damper, and open the stove door slightly for a minute or two, vents and sauna door closed. Small, not quite seasoned birch sticks give the desired fragrance, but try apple, cedar, or any other aromatic wood. After "smoking" the room in this fashion, open the damper, close the stove door, and fully vent the place for, say, five minutes or as required to purge the visible smoke. Finally, stoke the stove and close the vents and sauna door, allowing the room to return to the desired bath temperature. There will be no smoke left, but the fragrance of the smoke will remain.

Other fragrances are sometimes introduced at löyly time. Although purists may reject this relatively new (20th-century) custom, it is becoming more and more popular on both sides of the Atlantic. Various nostrums are mixed with the löyly water in small quantities, adding flavor to the sacred steam. Birch leaf essence is popular in some countries. Tom Johnson and Tim Miller (in their *Sauna Book*) advise mixing a few drops of "drugstore oil"—peppermint, spearmint, wintergreen, whatever—with a cup of water. Either put it in a tin can on top of the rocks or splash it on during the löyly process. Author and sauna expert Mikkel Aaland likes sage, basil, rosemary, or laurel bay ("Not too much, it's potent"). Tylo, the Swedish sauna equipment manufacturer, even sells "sauna oils" to zap the steam.

For a down-home aroma, Johnson and Miller report: "A mixture of several (say, four) parts of water to one part of beer, will, some claim, produce a smell like warm bread, while straight beer ladled directly onto the stones tends to smell more like burnt toast." I can personally vouch for the warm bread aroma with the splashing of a four-to-one hot water to beer noggin. It's pleasant enough for a while, but tastes a little of gimmickry.

Whatever potions you might come up with, use them sparingly or they can be a distraction from the real löyly spirit, which pure water creates extremely well.

How Long?

How long to stay in the sauna is, again, a matter best left to each individual, but neophytes should err on the side of caution. The sauna is emphatically not a place for endurance contests, even within oneself. Listen to your body clock. Years ago, in Scotland, a friend was bathing in my little cottage sauna, at about 160 degrees F. This was his first sauna, and he stayed in too long. On the way out the door he had to sit on the floor and hold his ankles to keep from fainting.

For the inexperienced bather with no idea at all of how long to stay in, a wide parameter would be 5 to 15 minutes for the first session, depending somewhat on temperature, but mostly on how the individual feels. If uncomfortable in any way, step outside. Even winter air is not hard to take directly from the sauna.

Cooling

Sweating is followed by cooling, which can take several different forms. Even 75-degree F. summer air will offer relief from the stoveroom, but it will not provide the desired contrast. In winter, when we use the sauna most, the outside air, typically o degrees to 20 degrees F., usually provides a good contrast. A little snow and wind also help. Writer Denise McCluggage enthuses, "If it is snowing, I walk out into the night of the deserted countryside and the flakes fall like a constant shower of tiny needles on my lifted arms." And McCluggage takes the snowy night experience to the next logical step. "The body is so stoked by the heat from the sauna that it steams in the cold air and melts deep molds of itself in the snow bank I drop into. Sweeping my arms at my sides, I imprint an angel shape, laughing to see the snow crystals dissolve on this griddle surface that is me."

Isn't that an awful shock to the system? Actually, it isn't. Fluffy snow is a very good insulation at about R-1 per inch, the same as wood. It drains the heat away from the body faster than cold air, because our bodies soon change the snow to water, but not as fast as total immersion in water, the fastest cooling method. (No one advises a head first plunge into the water, by the way, but neither should you creep in slowly. Take the plunge, but keep your head above water.)

Incidentally, the cool plunge, like the creation of good löyly, is another part of the sauna ritual that has not gained great popularity in the United States, possibly because most American saunas are not built in the classic Finnish country location, next to a lake or the sea. Or, we might just be more conservative.

Other means of rapid cooling, both used extensively by the Finns, are a cold shower and, commonly, pouring a bucket of cool water over one's body. We used to use a Solar Shower at Log End Sauna, but mostly for final washdown, not for cooling. It could be used for cooling, even in summer, if kept out of the sun. I often use the bucket routine, usually right in the stoveroom, as the water simply runs down the drain.

Whatever the method of cooling, best not overdo it. A chill from too long in the plunge pool is no better than feeling faint from too much heat.

Repeat

The next great and welcome contrast is the return to the stoveroom. Mmmmm! Back to the womb!

Alternating sessions in the heat with (generally shorter) sessions of cooling is the heart of the sauna experience. Go back and forth as long as it feels good. A number that pops up often in the literature—one that I tend to favor myself—is three; that is: three complete cycles of hot and cold. After that, I seem to run into the proverbial point of diminishing returns.

Whisking

In general, Americans seldom include löyly as a part of the sauna. They are even less inclined toward the pleasures of the plunge pool. But, I don't think I have heard of any American (at least of non-Finnish ancestry) who makes use of the birch whisk, or "vihta." And, if you want to know, a lot of sauna users in Finland don't use it either.

Yet use of the vihta is considered by many an essential part of the sauna ritual, so we had better find out what it's all about. Does the common perception of the steaming masochist delighting in self-flagellation have any relationship to reality? Well, it does. The main misconception here is that beating oneself with the whisk involves pain. Rather, the experience is described as a massaging of the skin, sometimes as a further stimulant to the blood flow. The vihta also helps remove the already loosened dead skin, although this shedding can also be accomplished with a coarse washcloth, loofah sponge, or pumice stone.

Sauna is a combination of sensory experiences, and whisking is a good example of this. There is the whishing sound as the whisk is swung, the sound of it slapping against the wet naked skin, the distinctive fragrance of the aromatic substances in the fresh birch leaves being released into the stoveroom. Viherjuuri enthuses that the tingling sensation caused by löyly is increased by beating with a whisk of birch leaves.

As previously stated, my study into sauna has greatly improved the quality of our sauna building itself, as well as our bathing methodology. In over 30 years of sauna experience, I had never tried the vihta, never even seen it in use. With my research papers for this book as a guide, Jaki and I made our first vihta and put it to use. By early July, most of the mature birch trees no longer had fresh young leafy shoots for making good vihtas; the little branches were already turning woody. I was reminded of an anecdote from sauna writer and architect Elmar Badermann, which tells of the use of birch whisks in Germany:

> I had told some friends about birch whisks, and they had promised to give them a try sometime. They later reported miserably how they had tried them out on a cold November day; they complained that the birch

7-2. *Jaki cuts a few young sprigs of birch to make a vihta.*

7-3. *Three strong elastic bands hold several sprigs together to make a handle for the vihta.*

whisks had been very painful. There is quite a difference between birch whisks and birch branches.

Fortunately, a young birch tree still had some excellent soft branches, and we cut enough 18- to 24-inch sprigs to make a good vihta. The literature showed how the sprigs of birch leaves could be tied together beautifully with twine or vine, but we found that three stout elastic bands, folded over a few times, did a great job with much less effort.

We stood the vihta in a vase of water for a week until sauna day. Then, with the sauna at 150 degrees Farenheit or so, we rather sheepishly tried it out. The first problem I encountered was that the vihta would tend to get caught up in the rafters during the long sweeping, swishing swing through the air. A slightly larger stoveroom or slightly smaller vihta would be needed. The next problem was that the birch leaves began to break up upon impact with the skin, showing the importance of using fresh sprigs. I remembered that most authorities tell of making the whisks just before entering the sauna. A week's standing in a vase of water didn't help. Still, Jaki, Darin, and I were having a great time and a lot of laughs. We found that outside the sauna, we could achieve the required swing, although it still takes considerable coordination to beat oneself on the back and backside.

I knew that sauna matrons in Finland would provide vihta beating as a part of their service, so Jaki and I figured we would try beating each other. This was definitely easier and more satisfying. A good beating, like a good tickle, is most enjoyable if administered by someone else. We began to experience the tingling sensation described by others, but this improved a great deal with our next effort a few weeks later, with our greater experience and fresh vihtas.

Sex and Sauna

If all this is starting to sound a little on the kinky side, I assure you that it isn't. Matrons resembling Cindy Crawford with a domineering sneer exist only in the minds of depraved writers. Decorum is maintained in the sauna at all times, even during whisking. Nakedness is simply a practical necessity, as any covering is a discomfort. In sauna, at temperatures ranging from 200 degrees in the stoveroom to 40 degrees in the plunge pool, there are subtle and ethereal pleasures that are far removed from sex.

If this book was intended solely for the Scandinavian market, any mention of sex and the sauna would be unnecessary. Part of the long

Finnish tradition is that sauna is enjoyed by men and women separately, except with the family, where mixed bathing is common. But, as the American attitude toward sex is rather more puritanical than in Scandinavia (resulting in greater curiosity, suggestion, suspicion, even voyeurism), I will try to clear up a few misconceptions here.

Though sex in the sauna is technically possible (far wilder venues have been reported), more comfortable sites are easily found. Actually, an old Finnish saying has it that "a woman is at her most beautiful an hour after the sauna." In light of today's almost puritanically oppressive mania for sexual sameness, such a statement might be considered sexist, so let's presume that it holds true for men as well as women. And, as the sauna relaxes the body while stimulating the skin, the best advice for the libidinously inclined is to wait until sauna is complete (including a proper cooldown) before commencing a different sort of heating up.

Behavior in the Stoveroom

The Finns have certain unwritten rules for proper behavior in the stoveroom, rules that have passed the test of the ages. Though they are unwritten, I'll have to write them down; otherwise, you won't know what they are. Unless you're Finnish. So:

- No music or loud noises.
- No gawking.
- No swearing.
- Have consideration for the comfort of others. (This works both ways: It is as wrong to subject a saunamate to frustratingly lukewarm temperatures as it is to parboil the poor soul.)
- "Bad thoughts and malicious talk are left outside the sauna," says Dr. P. Sorri of Tampere, Finland.

All these rules can be summed up in one, which (in Finland, at least) is this: In sauna, one behaves as if in church.

Some purists maintain that one shouldn't read, speak except as necessary, or even think in the sauna, but I find myself siding with the many enthusiasts who find the sauna to be conducive to fellowship, conversation, open-mindedness, and even expanded consciousness. As Dr. Sorri says, "The sauna is an excellent place for philosophizing and creative thinking."

State of Consciousness

I have had wonderful conversations in the sauna, with friends and with total strangers. It is easy to attribute this purely to the atmosphere, conviviality, and sense of fun that are all part of sauna. But I have another theory, suggested by Aldous Huxley's essays, "Doors of Perception" and "Heaven and Hell." According to Huxley, our brains, of necessity, have a "cerebral reducing valve" that prevents biologically useless material originating in our "Mind-at-Large" from spoiling concentration on the particular concerns of the moment. Imagine if we were constantly overwhelmed by the almost infinite memories and information stored in the backwaters of our minds. But, sometimes, it is useful to be able to tap into this Mind-at-Large, to make creative connections that we might not see otherwise. Huxley's essays point out a variety of methods by which this cerebral reducing valve can be bypassed, opening the "doors of perception" into a truly "open mind." Among these methods are fasting, strobe lights, sensory deprivation, various drugs (he describes his mescaline experience), and (the one that caught my attention) breathing air that is high in carbon dioxide.

In a small sauna, carbon dioxide (CO_2) levels might very well be higher than normal. The saunees are breathing in oxygenated air and expelling CO_2 gas. If ventilation is not keeping up with the shortfall, it is conceivable that a higher than normal ratio of CO_2 to oxygen might just let a few leaks of perception sneak around the cerebral reducing valve, resulting in a greater receptivity to different sorts of neural connections.

Unlike Huxley, I am not a scientist. But it's a free country and I'm entitled to my silly theories. I thought of this one while in the sauna. But read Dr. Sorri's comments below and see if they don't sound a lot like opening the "doors to perception." Maybe a real scientist (or a Finnish M.D.—they seem to delight in studies like this) can conduct tests on CO_2 content in the sauna.

Standard sauna wisdom is that the ventilation system should promote air changes at the rate of six per hour. How we are supposed to count these air changes is never explained. But ventilation should not be diminished in an attempt to promote higher consciousness, or the bather might find himself closer to unconsciousness, like my friend in Scotland.

Mikkel Aaland, in his excellent book *Sweat*, raises the possibility that the good feeling in a properly conditioned sauna might come from the creation of "negative ions" during löyly production. Studies have suggested that negative ions—molecules carrying a negative electrical charge—are better for our health and sense of well-being than positive ions. This is a large and somewhat controversial subject, and beyond the scope of this book. But, if you're a negative ion junkie, you'll know that combustion and crashing water are two ways that negative ions (the "good" ions) are produced. Mr. Aaland comments:

> The effect of negative ions on sweat bathing was discovered when researchers were trying to account for the tremendous popularity of sauna wood burning stoves over electric stoves. Subjective reasons, such as the fragrance of burned wood, did not fully explain why Finns felt so refreshed after time in a wood heated sauna and quite dulled, from certain electrically heated saunas.

The tests in Finland to which Mr. Aaland refers show that the löyly produced when water is splashed on very hot rocks greatly increases the incidence of negative ions, while the electric heater elements alone (think of the typical American hotel or YMCA sauna) can increase the preponderance of the adverse positive ions. Actually, savusaunas seemed to be best at producing negative ions, but "the ion distribution of air depends on the temperature of the stones in the kiuas." Again, it comes back to this: the hotter the rocks, the better the löyly. Are the spiritual qualities of löyly, described through the centuries, really a function of ion number count? Or sauna spirits? The mind boggles. But that's the idea.

Sauna and the Psyche

Dr. P. Sorri, in his article entitled "The Sauna and Bathing Habits: A Psychoanalytic Point of View," which appeared in *Annals of Clinical Research: Special Issue on Sauna*, makes the following observations, among others. Italics are mine.

- "Freedom from the limitations of everyday reality and rationality is a necessary prerequisite for a rich and vivid experience in the sauna. Sauna bathing tends to provoke such a state of mind. This demands a temporary, partial and reversible regression in the functions of the ego to developmentally earlier modes of functioning. These are characterised by *immediate experientiality, holisticity and easy access to feelings and fantasies.* This enables the subject to leave unnecessary criticism and rationality behind, and *allows his mind to be empowered by fantasies, emotions, and immediate sensations.*"

- "The harsh world feels miles away and *the bather lives in the here and now in the sauna.*"
- "The whole process of taking a sauna and its specific physical milieu promote a kind of *magic tuning*, which repels evil and dissolves the everyday stresses of life."
- "Many serious private and political problems have been constructively solved in sauna. Rationality and commonplace thinking are abandoned and replaced by a *positive disposition* and an inclination to understand other peoples' point of view thus *promoting creativity and a capacity to find new solutions.*"

Washing Down

After the final session of perspiration, a good washing down is in order before repairing to the relaxation room. Many aficionados on both sides of the Atlantic find a shower to be the most convenient method of removing the remaining sweat and dead skin. We used this method ourselves in Scotland and at our sauna inside Log End Cottage. Many indoor saunas are placed convenient to a shower for this purpose.

With a freestanding outdoor sauna, the complications of plumbing drive most people to some alternative washing-down procedure.

One suggestion, already mentioned, but worth a reminder here, is the use of a Solar Shower. This device, which can be purchased from Real Goods Trading Corporation (555 Leslie Street, Ukiah, CA 95482–5507), is a heavy-duty five-gallon plastic bag, clear on one side, black on the other. It works by solar energy and gravity. Fill it with water, hang it in the sun (from a pole, tree, or the front of a Log End-style sauna), and—for several months of the year at least, depending on climate—it will provide a warm shower for the final washdown with soap and a coarse washcloth or loofah sponge. A heavy plastic clip pinches the hose shut while the sun warms the water in the bag. Release of the clip allows the warmed water to reach the shower head. The clip also allows for flow adjustment.

The Solar Shower could be used in winter by simply bringing the bag of water up to the desired temperature in the stoveroom itself, and hanging it up outside just prior to use.

Since 1978, our preferred method of washdown is right in the sauna. We bring a bucket or two of water into the stoveroom itself, and store it on the floor, but out of the way of dripping sweat. We have found that two or three gallons of water for each bather is sufficient.

We also use this water for pouring on the rocks or bricks to create the löyly steam.

We scrub the loosened dead skin off the body with soap and a washcloth or loofah. It is a welcome courtesy to offer to scrub each other's backs. We always use a certain one-pint plastic pitcher to ladle the wash water out of the bucket. We never put a washcloth or soap in the bucket, or the water will not remain clean for the final rinse. After sudsing and shampooing, we rinse with several pints of water poured over the head. Sometimes, I will use warm water for washing and cool water for the final rinse.

I like to shave in sauna, and keep a mirror there for that purpose. I use the plastic pitcher as a shaving mug for rinsing the razor. Whiskers never come off so easily as after a good long sweat in the sauna.

Prior to leaving the stoveroom, I will use a couple of pitchers of water and the washcloth to rinse down the sweat-dampened parts of the platforms. If I am the last bather (I usually am) and there is water left in the bucket (there usually is), I enjoy pouring the remainder over my head. This is the perfect finish to the stoveroom visit. Cool water for this final rinse helps begin the cooling process which continues in the relaxation room. I gather up all the sauna paraphernalia (pitchers, drinking cups, washcloth, shaving stuff, shampoo, etc.) and put it in the empty bucket and remove it—and myself—to the relaxation room.

THE RELAXATION ROOM

The relaxation room and the dressing room can be one and the same, if good planning has made efficient use of space. Only the most ostentatious among us would designate separate chambers. In fact, before the 20th century, the Finns did not have a special room designated for either dressing or cooling down. As a relatively recent innovation (and a good one) there is considerable latitude as to its use. In summertime, or in the extreme south, an outdoor deck or patio—even a couple of benches in the grass or woods—will serve as well or better.

The Dry-Down

Authorities agree that the skin should dry naturally; it should not be toweled off. I can report, from experience, that toweling down too early is simply a waste of time. The body continues to perspire for several minutes after leaving the stoveroom. Towel immediately and you're wet again in five minutes. The evaporative effect of natural air drying promotes cooling of the body and slows perspiration. A final plunge in cool or cold water just before the relaxation room will also help by closing the pores and bringing the body mass temperature down, all of which assists in stopping those thousands of tiny leaks in the skin.

The relaxation room should not be too cool, or a chill or at least a discomfort will result. A temperature in the low 70s works for me. And, as in the stoveroom, a reclining position is a good place to start. If conditions are comfortable, a ten or fifteen minute lie-down after the sauna is a most relaxing experience. Remember that, aerobically, a sauna is not unlike a physical work-out. You need a rest.

You're dry when, according to an old Finnish maxim, "a leaf will fall off the skin by itself." My own rule isn't quite as poetic: "When you're dry, you're dry." Then it's time to dress.

I hope you brought a change of clothes.

Refreshment

After a natural cooldown and drying, the body craves a replenishment of fluids and salts left behind in the stoveroom. In Finland, a special sauna sausage is one of many delicacies used to break the fast. I find that any salty snack—pepperoni, cheese, and crackers are nice, for example—along with a good micro- or home-brewed ale, provides the perfect conclusion to the sauna. For the more health-conscious, mineral water and raw vegetables with humus or a spicy dip will taste great. In Finland, elaborate sauna meals are prepared in advance, sometimes with some of the dishes slow-cooked right in the stoveroom, with great care taken to prevent unwanted cooking odors from disturbing the proper sauna atmosphere. On the sauna platform, "eggs can be cooked hard without water," says Viherjuuri.

SAUNA IS A PERSONAL MATTER

I have tried in this chapter to present a variety of sauna use patterns and ideas, some of which have stood longer tests than others. It is not a complete list by any means, because everyone seems to create their own innovations, which become habits, and, if they're good, become a part of sauna lore, such as chimneys and relaxation/changing rooms around the turn of the century. How long did it take for beating with whisks to become a part of the sauna culture? Will flavoring the löyly with various potions become a regular part of the ritual, or remain an isolated or passing fancy? Are there new and positive developments (as opposed to negative ions) brewing in the mist?

Sauna is not the only means of sweat-bathing. Californian Mikkel Aaland, in *Sweat*, describes his three-year worldwide search for the perfect bath. He tells of his experiences in Turkish "hammams" (public sweat baths, some of them hundreds of years old), the Russian "bania" (which has a lot in common with sauna), various Japanese sweat baths (sauna is popular there), and even variations of the Native American sweat lodge ceremony. While sweating seems to be the common denominator, other patterns, such as variations on whisking, seem to have developed independently around the planet. For example, Mexicans in their sweat bath (called a "temescal" and dating from ancient Mayan times), use corn husks as vihtas. Perhaps some of these common threads date back to prehistory and intercontinental contact. We'll probably never know.

Be yourself. While the basic time-tested patterns and rituals of the Finnish tradition provide a can't-go-wrong starting point, you'll no doubt refine your bath to suit your own needs, whims, climate, and the building itself. I would caution against dogmatism in the sauna, but such a caution is probably redundant. Whether from CO_2, negative ions, or just the conviviality of sauna itself, open-mindedness seems to reign in the sauna. Sweat and enjoy.

West Chazy, New York
Bacalar, Mexico
Caye Caulker, Belize

Appendices

APPENDIX ONE

Sauna Equipment Manufacturers and Distributors

Except as noted, I have confined this list to suppliers of sauna heaters. Omission of any supplier here simply means that, despite following up on several different lists and sources, I was unable to learn of the supplier's existence during my research. Similarly, inclusion in this list should not be taken as an endorsement. While I have found the sauna industry representatives to be generally delightful to deal with, I have no personal experience with their products. Descriptions are based on information supplied, and supplemented by follow-up phone calls.

Write to these companies for their literature and price lists. And please enclose a dollar to cover their mailing expenses, as most of the literature comes in oversized envelopes. They will appreciate it, and you will get better attention. If you are building your own sauna, let them know up front. It will save time and unneeded glossy paper. Some questions you might want to ask are: How long has the company been in business? Are their heaters UL or CSA listed (if necessary for insurance purposes)? What are the recommended clearances around the heater? Where is the nearest dealer or showroom? What kind of warranty do the products carry, and for how long?

Sort through the information you receive, narrow the list to those suppliers that seem to offer the products that best suit your situation, and follow up with specific questions over the phone. Don't be afraid to bargain with the reps. I get the sense that very few premanufactured saunas or sauna heaters are sold at full retail price. Many suppliers will throw in sauna accessories with their bigger-ticket items.

The list is in alphabetical order. Remember that companies come and go and phone numbers change, particularly 800 numbers. The information given was checked for accuracy in May of 1996.

Amerec Products (Nasscor)

P.O. Box 40569, Bellevue, WA 98015; 206–643–7500, 800–331–0349; fax: 206–643–2124.

Manufactures full line of Amerec electric heaters from small 120-volt plug-in units for very small saunas right up to huge 15 Kw, 208-volt, three-phase and 240-volt single-phase heaters for giant saunas of 1,100 cubic feet capacity.

Amerec is America's major sauna heater manufacturer. All units are UL listed. Call for warranty information. They also make small personal sauna rooms, as well as medium-sized and large rooms. Amerec makes a precut sauna cabin made of 3 × 6 tongue-and-groove solid western cedar logs, as well as prehung sauna doors. They sell a full range of accessories. John Gunderson is helpful and knowledgeable.

Arctic Sauna and Steam Corporation
    25–27 Knowles Street, Yonkers, NY 10705; 914–423–0730.

Sells Polar electric heaters and Saunatec wood-fired heaters, both made by Helo in Finland. They also sell six different Saunatec wood-burning sauna stoves, some with attached water tanks.

BHS Sauna and Steam
    P.O. Box 1372, Riverhead, NY 11901; 516–727–9107, 800–447–2862.

Sells electric, wood, and gas-burning heaters, as well as Aito wood-burning heat storage stoves. BHS designs and builds Finnish and American-type saunas, outdoor solid wood-wall saunas, and sauna cottages. They also repair and provide parts for major heater brands. Vince Paladino, President of BHS, is one of sauna's real characters. He is a firm believer in the savusauna or "smoke sauna," and even offered to convert our Earthwood Sauna to a savusauna. Although I declined, I enjoyed a couple of long sauna conversations during which I learned about the state of the sauna industry and the (in Vince's view) particularly sorry state of sauna itself in the U.S. He feels strongly that we have wandered so far from the original sauna of Finland, that what is left is hardly recognizable as sauna.

The Aito woodstove from Finland is particularly interesting and seems to have very high performance characteristics, particularly with regard to the making of "löyly," the sacred sauna steam. The stones themselves can reach temperatures of 2,000 degrees Farenheit, but the upper part of the stove is insulated with rock wool and firebricks, so the heat remains "soft." Löyly is created by applying water to the stones through a shutter. Opening and closing this shutter regulates the temperature.

Bruce Manufacturing, Inc.
    Route 1, Box 25, Bruce Crossing, MI 49912; 906–827–3906.

Manufactures Nippa electric, gas, and wood-burning heaters. Nippa sauna stoves have been manufactured in Michigan's Upper Peninsula since 1930. All Nippa stoves carry a five-year warranty. Some of the wood-fired and gas models have an optional water tank or jacket. The gas models are among the more affordable units I was able to find, and the other stoves are also moderately priced. Owner Gil Kotila is helpful, knowledgeable, and friendly.

Cedarbrook Sauna and Steam USA

5455 Sunset Highway, P.O. Box 535, Cashmere, WA 98815; 509–782–2447, 800–634–6334; fax: 509–782–3680.

Sells Vico gas heaters (U.S.), Finnleo wood-burning stoves (Finland), Tylo electric heaters (Sweden), Polar electric heaters (Finland). All Tylo electric heaters and control panels are UL listed. Some models have the control panels built into the heater. With regard to Polar heaters, made by Helo, Cedarbrook says that similar units are manufactured under the following names: Narvi, Finnleo, Harvia. In addition to sauna rooms and accessories, Cedarbrook manufactures prehung sauna doors (with or without windows), which could be a very handy item for a do-it-yourselfer building a cordwood sauna. John Lysaker, with 19 years in the sauna industry, is very helpful. He tells me that they rarely sell a gas-fired heater, only occasionally for Alaskan hunting camps or for large commercial applications in places like Manhattan. "They are expensive and difficult to install," says John.

Fenno Manufacturing, Ltd.

461 Esna Drive, Unit 6, Markham, Ontario, Canada L3R 1H8; 905–475–0261 (voice and fax).

Manufactures Fenno electric heaters (5 models) and Fenno wood-burning stoves (8 models). Electric models are made to heat stoverooms from 162 to 540 cubic feet and are CSA listed. The wood-burning units are available with or without stainless steel water tanks. Fenno has been in business since 1944.

Finlandia Sauna

14010-B SW 72nd Ave., Portland, OR 97224–0088; 503–684–8289, 800–354–3342; fax: 503–684–1120.

Sells Finlandia electric stoves, made by Harvia in Finland, and Harvia wood-burning stoves. Both stoves from Harvia feature mostly stainless steel in the construction. The Harvia-16 wood-burner has a water tank option.

Finnish American Sauna

2384 Bay Road, Redwood City, CA 94063; 415–327–5001; fax: 415–364–6770.

Manufactures Finlander gas-fired sauna heaters. Finlander gas heaters have been manufactured since 1973 and UL listed since 1987. They are also approved by the American Gas Association (AGA). They will operate on natural gas, propane (LP) gas, butane, or even fuel oil. (The fuel-oil units are not UL listed.) Retail price in March of 1996 for the standard 45,000 BTU unit, suitable for a 300–500 cubic foot stoveroom, was about $2,700. Even the contractor's discount leaves the price over $1,800, not including shipping or chimney. The upside is that they are much cheaper to run than electric heaters, and would do well at remote sites where wood-burning is not allowed.

NeKen Saunas

7740 Main Street, N.E., Minneapolis, MN 55432; 612–574–1738.

Manufactures four sizes of NeKen electric sauna heaters. The two smaller ones, for stoverooms of 325 cubic feet and 450 cubic feet, are UL listed. Five-year warranty on workmanship and materials, and one year on components and moving parts.

ProLux Sauna and Steam

62 Hamel Road, Hamel, MN 55340; 612–478–3240; fax: 612–478–3241.

Sells Spartan gas sauna heaters (U.S.), Tylo electric heaters (Sweden), and Saunatec wood-fired sauna stoves (Finland). ProLux builds saunas, but they are also a major distributor for the Tylo line of heaters and accessories from Sweden. Some of the interesting Tylo items, besides their high-quality electric heaters, are prehung sauna doors, a hydraulic door closer, a variety of sauna-compatible electric lamps and shades, thermometers, hygrometers (for measuring humidity), and fragrances (such as eucalyptus, pine, and peppermint) for "flavoring" the löyly. Don Kariniemi is the gaffer.

Saunacore, Inc.

5 Colomba Drive, Suite #149, Niagara Falls, NY 14305–1275; in Canada, 71 Strada Drive #8, Woodbridge, Ontario, L4L 5V8; 800–361–9485 (in both Canada and the U.S.)

Manufactures Saunacore electric heaters. The Canadian-made Saunacore electric heaters are stainless steel construction and come with a five-year warranty on the elements and body. The thermostat, made by someone else, has a one-year warranty. A 9 Kw unit, made for saunas of about 450 cubic feet, was less than $600 in March of 1996. Another 9 Kw unit, with heavy-duty elements and a lifetime warranty, was about $100 more. The heaters are "made to UL standards" and are listed by CSA. Phillip (at the 800-number) is very helpful.

Saunamatic

P.O. Box 49758, Colorado Springs, CO 80949–9758; 719–260–9648, 800–472–8627; fax: 719–590–9454.

Sells Saunatec heaters from Finland, including Helo, Polar, and others.

Manufactures Saunamatic heaters through their Canadian affiliate, Canadian Sauna Sales, Ltd. Saunamatic provides nationwide delivery of prefabricated sauna rooms, precut materials kits, accessories, parts, and repair service. They offer installation in much of the United States. Saunamatic has sold and supported their products for over 25 years. Ron Chartier is the man to talk with.

Saunas by Erkki

7636 Shirley Blvd., Port Tobacco, MD 20677; 301–934–8737.

Sells Finnleo electric heaters (Finland); 24 models of heater, 6 models of controls. Lots of people know Erik (Erkki) Lindstrom as "the Sauna Man." Although he sells top-of-the-line Finnleo electric heaters, sauna rooms, and accessories, Erkki himself is a traditional wood-fired sauna advocate. He has been building personalized saunas coast to coast for 30 years, including a log sauna for the Finnish embassy.

Saunatec, Inc.

575 East Cokato St., Cokato, MN 55321; 612–286–5584 (Saunatec); 800–882–4352 (Helo); 800–346–6536 (Finnleo).

Imports Helo and Finnleo electric heaters (Finland), and Saunatec wood-burning heaters (Finland). Saunatec is the parent of two "sister" companies: Helo Sauna and Finnleo Sauna and Steam, both at the same Cokato address. Saunatec is the American importer for both Helo and Finnleo sauna rooms and electric sauna heaters, two of the world's largest selling brands. Both are UL listed. Saunatec licenses various dealers around the U.S. They also sell a full line of sauna accessories: wooden buckets, ladles, thermometers, hygrometers, and lots of nice wooden things like headrests and duck boards that would be easy to make yourself. One of their more interesting offerings is the Helo Porta-Saun, which comes complete in two pieces and fits through any standard doorway. With finished outside dimensions just 45 inches wide by 45 inches deep by 77 inches high, and the ability to plug into an ordinary 15- or 20-amp outlet, this is a nice little two-person sauna cabinet that can fit in an existing space in the house. While not quite the full authentic sauna experience, the Porta-Saun might be of value to apartment dwellers.

Spartan Sauna Heaters, Inc.

7484 Malta Road, Eveleth, MN 55734; 218–741–8433.

Manufactures Spartan electric, wood, and gas-fired heaters. Imports Saunacore electric heaters from Canada (CSA listed). The Spartan electric sauna heater comes in four different sizes for both floor and wall installation. The Spartan gas model, around $850 in 1996, needs no electric connections and will heat up to 500 cubic feet. The Spartan wood-fired stoves accommodate 200 pounds of rocks. One of the wood-fired models has a 25-gallon nonpressurized water tank, a nice feature. Spartan has been in the sauna business since 1953. Ted Heikkinen was very helpful on the phone. Like other suppliers, he says that the gas models are not popular.

U.S. Sauna and Steam

9 Cross Street, Norwalk, CT 06851; 203–846–9192, 800–243–6764.

Sells 19 different Polar electric heaters (made by Helo in Finland) to serve any stoveroom from a sauna closet of 70 cubic feet to a party room of 950 cubic feet. All are UL-listed.

Vico Industries

1808 Patrero, South Elmonte, CA 91733; 800–262–2588.

Manufactures Vico gas sauna heaters, which are distributed by Cedarbrook Sauna and Steam USA.

Pre-cut sauna room with Amerec electric corner heater (Amerec Products).

Appendix Two
Sauna Societies

Sauna-Seura r.y. (The Finnish Sauna Society), Vaskiniemi, SF-00200 Helsinki 20, Finland. As most of the saunas in the world are probably still in Finland, The Finnish Sauna Society can be considered the leading society of its kind in the world.

Sauna Society of America, 1001 Connecticut Ave., Washington, DC 20036. V. S. Choslowsky, Executive Director, tells me: "Currently, the activities of the Society are limited to public information services, disseminating information to the general public and offering various publications on the subject of the sauna. Lists of sauna concerns or operators are no longer maintained." The Society distributes some very useful books on sauna, listed in the bibliography. Further, Mr. Choslowsky says, "There is a dearth of simple and useful publications in the marketplace, dealing with easy-to-follow, step-by-step instructions to build a functional sauna for the do-it-yourself enthusiast, no matter what method or materials are used. While we are not familiar with your 'cordwood' sauna concept, we trust that it incorporates the #1 requirement for any true and authentic sauna: fresh air! Cool, fresh air must be allowed to enter and 'used' hot air must be allowed to escape—by convection—for any sauna to be pleasant and enjoyable." The walls of a cordwood sauna, in my view, breathe better than any other kind, and it is easy to incorporate additional venting as needed.

APPENDIX THREE
Annotated Bibliography

CORDWOOD MASONRY, EARTH ROOFS

In August of 1996, these books—and video—were available from Earthwood Building School, 366 Murtagh Hill Road, West Chazy, NY 12992, which acts as a national clearinghouse for information on cordwood masonry and earth-sheltered housing.

Nash, George, *Do-It Yourself Housebuilding: The Complete Handbook*, Sterling Publishing Co., Inc., New York, 1994. Everything about building, except cordwood masonry and earth roofs: foundations, framing, electrical, plumbing, finishing, ad infinitum. This huge book (over 3½ pounds of paper) is the best single how-to building reference work I have found. 704 pages, 1771 photos and diagrams.

Roy, Rob, ed. *Cococo/94 Collected Papers*, Earthwood Building School, West Chazy, New York, 1994. This is the complete transcription of all twenty-five papers written for the 1994 Continental Cordwood Conference in West Chazy, N.Y. Topics are grouped under four headings: Technical Papers, Code Issues, Case Studies, and Historical. 170 pages.

Roy, Rob, *Complete Book of Cordwood Masonry Housebuilding: The Earthwood Method*, Sterling Publishing Co., Inc., New York, 1992. The book covers the three styles of cordwood masonry construction: as infilling within a post-and-beam frame, with curved walls, and with stackwall (built-up) corners. Eighteen illustrated case studies are included. The second part of the book details the construction of the Earthwood house. 264 pages, 290 illustrations, 8 pages in color.

Roy, Rob, *The Complete Book of Underground Houses: How to Build a Low-Cost Home*, Sterling Publishing Co., Inc., New York, 1994. Post-and-beam and plank-and-beam methods of construction are featured, as well as surface-bonded block walls, and all aspects of the earth roof. 148 pages, 150 illustrations, 19 in color.

Roy, Rob, and Jaki Roy, *Basic Cordwood Masonry Techniques*. This 88-minute video is a mini-course in cordwood masonry. It shows barking the wood, mixing the mortar, building the cordwood walls, pointing, laying up window frames, attaching door frames, and stackwall corner construction. It discusses types of wood and how long to dry them, estimating quantities, and special design effects. Available from Chelsea Green Publishing Company, White River Junction, VT.

Shockey, Cliff, *Stackwall Construction: Double Wall Technique*, Huerto Publishing Company, Vanscoy, SK, 1993. Cliff shares his highly energy-efficient cordwood design, which consists of separate inner and outer cordwood walls, with fiberglass insulation and a vapor barrier between. This is truly a superinsulated wall-building technique. Cliff has built a cordwood masonry sauna in cold Saskatchewan. 80 pages.

SAUNA

Most of the books on sauna are out of print. Look for the books and articles below at libraries and second-hand book stores. Those distributed by the Sauna Society of America are available from them. Their address is 1001 Connecticut Ave., Washington, DC 20036.

Aaland, Mikkel, *Sweat*, Capra Press, Santa Barbara, CA 93101, 1978. This large, beautifully illustrated and comprehensive volume is probably the most complete book ever done on the various baths that humankind has devised to promote sweat without work. The author describes in detail his three-year worldwide journey in search of sweat. The subtitle on the frontispiece says it all: "The illustrated history and description of the Finnish Sauna, Russian Bania, Islamic Hammam, Japanese Mushi-buro, Mexican Temescal, and American Indian & Eskimo Sweat Lodge." The book concludes with a fine chapter entitled "Build Your Own Sweat Bath" including 26 pages of good suggestions and illustrations about sauna. It's a shame that this book is out of print. 252 pages.

Badermann, Elmar, "Aesthetic and Physiological Sensory Perceptions in the Original Finnish Sauna," *Sauna Studies*, Papers read at the VI International Sauna Congress in Helsinki, August 15–17, 1974. The Finnish Sauna Society, Helsinki, 1976.

Berinstein, Dorothy, "Myths & Facts About Saunas," *Good Housekeeping*, March 1995.

Cowan, Tom, and Jack Maguire, *Spas & Hot Tubs, Saunas & Home Gyms*, Creative Homeowner Press, Upper Saddle River, NJ 07458, 1988. The 37-page section on saunas is quite good, with a lot of clear how-to illustrations and some good planning ideas. I found my copy in a second-hand book store.

Graeffe, Gunnar, et al. "The Ions in Sauna Air," *Sauna Studies*, Papers read at the VI International Sauna Congress in Helsinki, August 15–17, 1974. The Finnish Sauna Society, Helsinki, 1976.

Herva, Marjatta, *Let's Have a Sauna*, Sauna-Seura r.y. (The Finnish Sauna Society), Helsinki, Finland, distributed by the Sauna Society of America (undated). This booklet, illustrated with cartoons, is touted as "a humorous look at the origins, mores, benefits, and enjoyment of the Finnish bath." Written for the neophyte. I keep my copy in the sauna for guests to peruse. 24 pages.

Hollander, Carlton, *How to Build a Sauna*, Drake, New York, 1978. This long out-of-print book covers the basics of building a framed insulated sauna outdoors, or a built-in sauna room for indoor use. 128 pages.

Johnson, Tom, and Tim Miller, *The Sauna Book*, Harper and Row, New York, 1977. Here is a big, lavish, well-illustrated, and enthusiastically written book by a couple of real sauna enthusiasts. While out of date on sauna suppliers, the book is useful for its many money-saving do-it-yourself tips and devotes several interesting pages to North American sweat lodge lore. Above all, the book is a lot of fun. I found it through interlibrary loan, but grab it if it shows up in a used-book store. 198 large pages.

Luoma, Jon R., "Taking the Heat," *Audubon*, January 1987.

McCluggage, Denise, "The Sauna Experience," *American Home*, February 1971.

McCommons, James, "Build a Simple Sauna Retreat," *Country Journal*, Nov.-Dec. 1993.

S.A.K., "Hot Stuff," *Architectural Record*, April 1992.

Sauna and Your Health: Annals of Clinical Research. Finnish Medical Society, distributed in the U.S. by Sauna Society of America, 1988. Sixteen articles on the health benefits and concerns of sauna bathing. Some of the articles are highly technical and almost esoteric, but I found some to be quite useful and interesting. At $17.50, I would recommend this small book only for the serious researcher. 80 pages.

Sauna Studies, Sauna-Seura r.y. (The Finnish Sauna Society), Helsinki, Finland, distributed by the Sauna Society of America, 1976. This collection of professional papers from the 6th International Sauna Congress of 1974 is a fine reference volume on the technical, medical, architectural and historical aspects of sauna. There is even an illustrated article entitled "Sauna in Finnish Pictorial Art." While not a how-to book, the collection is indispensible for the serious sauna researcher. 301 pages.

Smith, Red, "Good Clean Fun in Finland," *Reader's Digest*, June 1968.

Sorri, P., "The Sauna and Sauna Bathing Habits: A Psychoanalytic Point of View," *Annals of Clinical Research: Special Issue on Sauna* 20, no. 4, The Finnish Medical Society, Helsinki, 1988.

Teeri, Niilo, "The Climatic Conditions of the Sauna," *Sauna Studies,* Papers read at the VI International Sauna Congress in Helsinki, August 15–17, 1974. The Finnish Sauna Society, Helsinki, 1976.

Vaha-Eskeli, K., (M.D.), and R. Erkkola, "The Sauna and Pregnancy," *Annals of Clinical Research: Special Issue on Sauna* 20, no. 4, The Finnish Medical Society, Helsinki, 1988.

Valtakari, P., "The Sauna and Bathing in Different Countries, *Annals of Clinical Research: Special Issue on Sauna* 20, no. 4, The Finnish Medical Society, Helsinki, 1988.

Viherjuuri, H. J., *Sauna: The Finnish Bath*, The Stephen Green Press, Brattleboro, VT, 1965. Viherjuuri has been called "the father of modern Sauna" and the book was long considered the bible of the subject, at least in America, where it was for many years the only work available in English. Many articles and books (including this one) quote from Viherjuuri, who is particularly strong on sauna history, folklore, customs, and proper use. There is not very much practical information on building a sauna or about stoves. 88 pages.

Vuori, Ilkka, M.D., "Healthy and Unhealthy Sauna Bathing," *Annals of Clinical Research: Special Issue on Sauna* 20, no. 4, The Finnish Medical Society, Helsinki, 1988.

Vuori, Ilkka, M.D., "Sauna Bather's Circulation," *Annals of Clinical Research: Special Issue on Sauna* 20, no. 4, The Finnish Medical Society, Helsinki, 1988.

Ylikahri, R., E. Heikkonen, and A. Suokas, "The Sauna and Alcohol," *Annals of Clinical Research: Special Issue on Sauna* 20, no. 4, The Finnish Medical Society, Helsinki, 1988.

APPENDIX FOUR
Glossary of Finnish Sauna Terms

kauha, kippo: dippers used for ladling water on to the konnos to make löyly

kiuas: the sauna stove, deriving from the original stone-built hearth

kiulu: a traditional wooden pail used in the sauna

konnos: rocks heated over the fire; they supply the "soft" heat for the sauna and will turn water into löyly

lauteet: the sauna platform

löyly: the hot sacred steam of the sauna

pesuhuone: washing room

riittaa jo!: hot enough!

sauna: the bathhouse itself; in Finland, the bathing experience itself is called kylpy

saunoa: to take a bath in the sauna

savusauna: smoke sauna

vasta, vihta: whisk made of birch, cedar, oak, or other small branches

Index

Chelsea Green Publishing Company

The sustainable world is one in which all human activities are designed to co-exist and cooperate with natural processes, rather than dominate nature. Resources are recognized to be finite. Consumption and production are carefully and consciously balanced so that all of the planet's species can thrive in perpetuity.

Chelsea Green specializes in providing the information people need to create and prosper in such a world.

Sustainable Living has many facets. Chelsea Green's celebration of the sustainable arts has led us to publish trend-setting books about organic gardening, solar electricity and renewable energy, innovative building techniques, regenerative forestry, local and bioregional democracy, and whole foods. The company's published works, while intensely practical, are also entertaining and inspirational, demonstrating that an ecological approach to life is consistent with producing beautiful, lucid, and useful books, videos, and audio tapes.

For more information about Chelsea Green, or to request a free catalog, call (800) 639–4099, or write to us at P.O. Box 428, White River Junction, VT 05001.

Chelsea Green's bestselling titles include:

The New Organic Grower	Eliot Coleman
Beyond the Limits	Meadows, Meadows, and Randers
Loving and Leaving the Good Life	Helen Nearing
The Contrary Farmer	Gene Logsdon
Solar Gardening	Leandre and Gretchen Poisson
Forest Gardening	Robert Hart
Who Owns the Sun	Berman, O'Connor
Whole Foods Companion	Dianne Onstad
The Flower Farmer	Lynn Byczynski
The Independent Home	Michael Potts
The Straw Bale House	Steen, Steen and Bainbridge
The Rammed Earth House	David Easton
Independent Builder	Sam Clark
The Passive Solar Home	Jim Kachadorian